# Modern
## meditations

## About the Author

Murray du Plessis started his meditation journey in 1997 and later spent ten years teaching meditation in England, South Africa, Burundi, and Namibia before moving to South Korea, where he now lives. He holds a master's degree in education and is an assistant professor of English at Daegu University. He has made eight trips to India on spiritual retreats, deepening his meditation practice in the Aravali Range of Rajasthan. His love for nature, outdoor adventure, and contemplation lead him regularly to Spain and Portugal, where he has done four Camino trekking pilgrimages—the ultimate moving meditation! You can be sure he's planning his next Camino right now.

MURRAY DU PLESSIS

# Modern
# meditations

## 101 Ways to
## *Slow Down & Connect*
## to Spirit

Llewellyn Publications
Woodbury, Minnesota

FIRST EDITION
First Printing, 2021

Cover design by Shannon McKuhen

Llewellyn Publications is a registered trademark of Llewellyn Worldwide Ltd.

**Library of Congress Cataloging-in-Publication Data**
Names: Du Plessis, Murray, author.
Title: Modern meditations : 101 ways to slow down & connect to spirit / Murray du Plessis.
Description: First edition. | Woodbury, Minnesota : Llewellyn Publications, 2021.
Identifiers: LCCN 2021005087 (print) | LCCN 2021005088 (ebook) | ISBN 9780738768359 | ISBN 9780738768571 (ebook)
Subjects: LCSH: Meditations.
Classification: LCC BL624.2 .D8 2021  (print) | LCC BL624.2  (ebook) | DDC 204/.35—dc23
LC record available at https://lccn.loc.gov/2021005087
LC ebook record available at https://lccn.loc.gov/2021005088

Llewellyn Publications
A Division of Llewellyn Worldwide Ltd.
2143 Wooddale Drive
Woodbury, MN 55125-2989
www.llewellyn.com

Printed in the United States of America

# Contents

# Introduction

Welcome, fellow truth seekers, to the realm of happiness, healing, and love. This is the world where *we* take the initiative to bring light and abundance into our lives instead of passively waiting for others to fill the gaps. We are the inner adventurers, the mystical pioneers, the dreamers of a better world. We know what we want, and we're willing to put the effort in to get there.

In our quest for meaning and exploration of spirit, we've no doubt read our fair share of self-improvement books, each one hopefully pointing us in the right direction and whetting our appetites for more. But in my experience, there just hasn't been that nuts-and-bolts compendium of guided meditations that takes the reader to the heart of it all, with limited distraction. And so, to fulfill that role, this book was born!

A warning: in this book, we'll be getting practical ... and I mean *practical*!

If you're expecting a book you can read from cover to cover in a week without much energy investment, you'll be disappointed.

If, however, you're in search of something that prompts you to find meaning, to dig for experiential growth on every page, you may well have stumbled upon what you were looking for. This book is going to get you meditating, I promise. Are you ready for the ride?

*Modern Meditations* is divided into twelve chapters, each one covering a different spiritual field. Within each field, you'll find a series of related meditations. If you wake up with a burning desire for change, head over to the chapter entitled "Transformation." If all you're after is some relaxation, there's a chapter for that, too, as well as for healing the self, celebrating abundance, and engaging with spirit. Simply find the chapter and the meditation that catches your eye, and then dive right in.

All in all, there are 101 guided meditations—or, alternatively stated, 101 loving conversations with yourself. That's as complicated as meditation needs to be—time spent in gentle conversation with yourself. The result? Something profoundly revealing, to say the least.

The meditations cover everything, from simple relaxation exercises, to creative visualizations; from walking meditations in nature, to explorations of otherworldly dimensions; from exercises in self-healing, to those that heal the world. They offer simple yet colorful pathways into spirituality, revealing how life can indeed be lived in a peaceful, meditative way.

## A Word on Thoughts

Thoughts, while possibly being our greatest asset, are sadly the one thing we squander the most. Think about it; they are the one thing constantly at our disposal in unlimited quantities. They have the power, in an instant, to uplift us—or, conversely, to bring us down. By being more mindful of our thinking—more aware of the energy we allow to flow through our minds—we can maneuver our life precisely, and quickly, and *consciously* in the direction we wish to go. Talking to ourselves in a loving, purposeful way enables us to build an inner environment filled with beauty and strength. One simple thought, said slowly and with conviction, can and *will* take us to an entirely new level of consciousness.

"I feel a glow in my heart, and it radiates outward, spreading warmth." Say this sentence again, slowly, patiently—and this time, with *conviction*. "I feel a glow in my heart, and it radiates outward, spreading warmth."

Did you feel something stir inside? I bet you did.

Spirituality can be—and inherently is—this simple. It's about cultivating and sustaining a beautiful inner environment, a garden within that flourishes with each positive thought we feed it. And when our hearts are warm and full, the world around us becomes an infinitely more special place to be in. Such is the power of positive self-talk. Such is the simplicity of spirituality.

## What Is Meditation?

Every book, and every teacher, no doubt has their own definition of meditation. So, what do *you* understand it to be?

Meditation can be simply sitting quietly and allowing your body to relax. It can be listening to your breathing and, in so doing, bringing yourself into the present. It can be an inner exploration as you direct your gaze, your focus, inward. It can be observing and cultivating your inner beauty, perhaps even experiencing that slice of perfection as you stumble upon a hidden jewel. It can be connecting to your inner flow of energy as you get in touch with the very vibration of life. It can be a pursuit of profound healing as you move yourself toward wholeness. It can be an exercise in developing a deeper understanding of yourself and, in doing so, deepening your understanding of others, too. It can be an appreciation of and connection to nature, life, and the universe. And it can be communion with God.

Meditation is, of course, all of the above—and more. It is both a journey inward into our unlimited inner world and a journey outward into the boundless outer world—and thus, by definition, a practice infinite in its scope.

One common theme in meditation is that it leads us to a greater awareness and understanding of the self. It takes us a little closer to answering that perennial question: *Who am I?* By reducing mental chatter and thus offering us a still, stable platform, meditation allows us to focus on and appreciate the simple beauty of the present. And it's in the stillness of the present where we can start sensing our inner life force. By being alert to this moment alone, the now, we can explore the very energy keeping us conscious and alive. We can uncover the mystical *I* existing at the center of our being.

Meditation, by initiating that inquiry into *self*, guides us to a better understanding of our body, our emotions, our mind, and our spirit, and by understanding ourselves holistically, we invariably improve our understanding of the world. Meditation could be considered absolute education; our minds become the laboratory in which we experiment with and learn about ourselves—and life.

The more active A-type personalities among us—you're out there, I know!—may sometimes feel meditation is just too passive, a repetitive activity that can regress into something boring and ineffectual, wasting our most precious resource: time. But meditation should never become stale and forced or in any way regimented; it can be as dynamic and creative as we wish. It's a journey—an adventure!—we undertake through the power of the mind. Each meditation can be as different and transcendent as we want it to be. Think an uplifting thought (*any* uplifting thought), take a moment to reflect on it, then embrace the beautiful feelings that emerge. Thoughts, accompanied by feelings and experiences, are what take us toward realization and truth.

Meditation gives us that platform to experiment with those very thoughts, feelings, and experiences and, in so doing, allows us to venture way outside the box. The inner journey of meditation is limited by our imagination alone—and our imagination, as we know, is without limitation! The universe of the mind is indeed a world without boundaries.

Meditation, of course, has a strong healing component, too. It puts us in touch with that deep, spiritual power we all possess yet often neglect. It allows us to tap into this inner force, awakening it and directing it to areas of our life that need healing. It may be that we are stressed out, or experiencing relationship or health problems, or have a yearning to understand ourselves and the world more completely. Regardless of where we feel out of sync or impaired in some way, meditation enhances our awareness of our inner environment, allowing us to take that first step into self-healing and self-transformation.

So, while meditation gives us the power to heal ourselves, it also brings healing to the world around us. By focusing within on our spiritual nature and exploring its innate beauty, we automatically start emitting that energy outward. Bringing positive influence into our surrounds no longer becomes a chore, but a natural expression of a full heart. When we're shining, our environment starts to shine, too. As they say, be the change you wish to see! Meditation is about exploring our virtues, too. In the midst of busy lives and even busier minds, aspects like peace, happiness, and love aren't always given the space and energy to flourish. Meditation leads us back to these reservoirs of goodness that—although often in a dormant, even abandoned state—are very much present inside us. It enables us to rekindle our spiritual light, sparking our inner world back to life as the jewels in the shadows start to shine again. And what greater healer is there—both for us and for the world—than a dose of peace, happiness, and love!

When we learn to merge meditation with our lives, our worlds become infinitely brighter and more meaningful. Everyday actions, no matter how menial they may be, can be infused with wonder, transforming the ordinary into something profound. And don't we all wish for a little wonder in our worlds!

## How to Use This Book

To access meditative states, we first need to ensure our body is relaxed; a restful body is, after all, key to achieving a restful mind. The first six meditations in this book focus on physical relaxation. The remaining meditations, for the sake of brevity, don't strictly include a relaxation component; nonetheless, it's always useful to start every meditation with a short relaxation exercise. With practice, calming the body can be achieved in a matter of seconds, be it via an inner body scan; a few deep, conscious breaths; humming several Oms; or a visualization exercise in which you take your mind to a peaceful place.

Gentle music, too, can be a useful aid in enabling deeper states. If you're not sure whether music or silence is a better fit for your meditation, experiment. Put on a soothing track that won't unduly distract you, then choose a meditation from the book and settle into it with an attitude of, "Ah, now this is surreal!" You may find music is just the catalyst that gets you in the mood.

So, how strictly should you follow each guided meditation? In answering this, we need to remember that guided meditations are simply a support structure, leading us onto that inward path. They *guide* us to a place of positivity and radiance. But it is your mind, not the words in the book, that will take you there. And so it may be that, as you sink deeper into one of the meditations, you find yourself in your own flow, on your own path, created through your own inner dialogue. Indeed, words may even become superfluous, with feelings alone fueling your experience. At this point, abandon the commentary, or alter it as you see fit, and venture off on your unique journey toward beauty and meaning.

Another tip is to not rush through any meditation. Society has oriented us toward getting results, with the fruits of our labor being considered more important than the process of moving in that direction. Meditation is different in that the process of doing it leads to no distinct destination; there is no limit to the depths of happiness we can experience, after all. This means we can keep enjoying that very process as we dive deeper in, and deeper still. Meditation is about being patient and enjoying that feeling of patience. It's about planting a seed, then observing the miracle of life that emerges. And in this space of quiet observation, feelings and experiences—life—*will* emerge.

Meditation is about acknowledging that this moment, right now, is good … indeed, perfect. Be patient, and you'll start to witness that glow of perfection, firsthand.

Now that we're on the topic of patience, my suggestion is to read each meditation's text as slowly and consciously as possible, even repeating parts if necessary. Move on to the next sentence only once you have felt and *become* the essence of the words—i.e., entered the experience. Experience is the key to long-lasting learning and growth. Remember, it's not about getting to the end of the meditation, it's about enjoying the experience, now.

In the meditations, I purposefully use the first person *I* in denoting *you*, the meditator, to encourage a more personal experience. For example:

"I take myself to a place of stillness within."

That feels better than "You take yourself to a place of stillness within," right?

So, what's better for meditation—eyes open, or closed?

This question is an interesting one. For many, the image meditation brings to mind is that of a yogi, eyes closed and silently seated in the lotus position. But meditation, of course, is not limited to that. It can be something we do while living life, interacting with others, walking in the forest, singing songs, or even playing sports. With a little practice, it can be something we integrate into our lives, bringing enjoyment and meaning to everything we do as we experience the beautiful coexistence of our inner and outer worlds. For this reason, learning to meditate with your eyes open can be a very useful lifestyle tool. Indeed, there are some meditations in this book that call specifically for this open-eyed approach.

If you prefer closed eyes—or for those meditations that *do* suggest closed eyes—there are several ways we can approach the obvious problem of having to read the guided meditation without the use of our eyes!

1. Read one sentence, then close your eyes. Give yourself as much time as you need to experience what you've just read. When you're ready, gently open your eyes, and move on to the next sentence before closing your eyes again. Again, I'd like to emphasize meditation's core tenet: patience. *Remind* yourself to be patient. Move slowly through the meditation, sentence by sentence, experience by experience, and before you know it, you'll be off and away!

2. Memorize the essence of the meditation. Then, in your own time, take yourself quietly through it, with eyes closed, via your own internal conversation. This memorizing technique is also useful for those meditations incorporating physical activity, such as walking or interacting with others, where reading the meditation in that moment wouldn't be possible. Another technique for the activity-based meditations is to simply *visualize* yourself doing the action. Within the wonderworld of your mind, you can be talking to your colleague, or walking down that very forest path the meditation refers to, absorbing those gorgeous rays of sunlight—even if it *is* raining outside!

3. Get together with friends and have one person read the meditation while the rest listen and follow. That's right;

make your own meditation club! And don't forget to invite me ... I'd love to join!

4. Metaphorically close your eyes. In other words, simply *pretend* your eyes are closed, giving yourself the sensation of closed eyes. Don't worry—it's not as tricky as it sounds!

5. If you're feeling ambitious, record yourself speaking these meditations—set to soothing music—and create your very own meditation audiobook!

## Soul and God

Although *soul* and *God* are components of some of the meditations, this book has no religious affiliations. It was written simply as a guide to rediscovering our original potential, that beauty and wisdom we all hold within. By occasionally bringing *soul* or *God* into our meditations, I believe we can enhance this feeling of beauty while opening the door to even deeper learning and realizations.

Also, this book is not prescriptive about who God is or isn't; we all have our own thoughts on this, after all. For the sake of consistency, I've gone with the name *God*, but if you're not comfortable with that title, feel free to substitute it with another, be it Mother, Father, Spirit, the Supreme, or the Divine. Also, God—mostly represented in these meditations as sacred light—is referred to in the feminine, using the pronoun *she*. This was done to emphasize those attributes more often ascribed to feminine divinity, like love, peace, and healing—all being such vital antidotes to some of the violence and pain we see happening in our world today.

My wish in writing this book is for us, the readers—regardless of our individual backgrounds—to enjoy the process of meditation as we continue to deepen our understanding and experience of spirituality. By spending time in the awareness of our bright inner worlds, we will automatically bring peace, happiness, and spiritual love into our lives and contribute toward a world we all wish to see. We heal ourselves, we heal the world. As we grow, so the world grows.

May each one of you find that special light-filled space within and share it with our world, inspiring others to find their own shining light. Enjoy the meditations. Be open, be free, and, most importantly, be patient and loving with yourself. Let goodness flow within, let beauty flourish, and make this moment, now, the best moment ever.

# Chapter 1
# Relaxation

Relaxation is about more than being chilled out; it's about being *at peace*. It's about steady breathing, a comfortable body, and a calm mind. It's about being present in our body and feeling content.

It's also the first step to a good meditation.

Are you relaxed right now? Check your body and find those tension spots. Breathe into them … and release. Slow down and become still. Ah, that's better. *Now* we're ready for some meditation!

## Becoming Heavy, Warm, and Relaxed

Thanks to sleep, our bodies get an extended daily break. But sleep isn't the only pathway to rejuvenation. By simply sitting down and consciously bringing our body into a "dormant" state, our muscles are given a chance to release all that tension they have a habit of holding on to. So, let's do just that and give our overworked bodies some time. To just. Relax.

Is your breathing smooth and slow? Is your body warm and at peace? Are your eyes content and smiling gently?

Admittedly, a lot of our stress may well have psychological and emotional components, making deep relaxation seem difficult. But for now, let's focus purely on the body. Let's look at the *physicality* of what is stopping us from being relaxed.

The reality is, we do hold tension, often unconsciously and unnecessarily, in our muscles—even when we're horizontal! What's needed is a gradual release, and one such method, progressive muscle relaxation (PMR), involves a mental check of our body, starting from our toes and moving slowly upward to our scalp, easing and relaxing each muscle group in turn.

With practice, PMR can be done in an instant via a quick internal body scan. The result is a relaxed, feel-good, energized body equipped to carry us forward in life.

———

Sitting comfortably or lying down, I focus on my breath. As I follow this cycle of inhalation and exhalation, I allow my breathing to slow down, to become deeper with each successive breath. With each in-breath, I take oxygen-rich air to the deepest reaches of my stomach, then release it slowly as I breathe out. I spend several moments doing just this: slow, deep inhalations followed by slow, deep exhalations. I turn my attention toward my toes now and breathe into them. I take my breath, very consciously, into the tips of each toe, and I watch as the air circulates there. As I breathe out, I say to myself, "My toes are becoming heavy, warm, and relaxed."

I repeat this, breathing into my toes, and out: "My toes are becoming heavy, warm, and relaxed."

I now move to the soles of my feet, breathing into them. And as I breathe out, I say, "The soles of my feet are becoming heavy, warm, and relaxed."

Once satisfied that they are indeed relaxed, I move up from there, doing the same for my ankles, my calves, my knees, my thighs, my buttocks, my stomach, my chest, my shoulders, my arms, my hands, my fingers, my back, my neck, my mouth, my eyes, my forehead, and, finally, my scalp.

As I move through each part of my body, I leave it in a calm and rested state. I leave it heavy, warm, and relaxed. I observe my body in its entirety now, noticing how settled it is, how comfortable it feels. I truly am heavy, warm, and relaxed. I now breathe into the vastness of my body, into its full expanse, before releasing the air in a long, slow, satisfied exhalation. At the same time, I feel my whole body letting go. And this letting go ... it feels so good.

My breathing continues to flow naturally, flow freely, flow easily. It is slow and deep. My body is dormant, at peace. In this restful state, I sense how my body is being recharged, how it is moving toward renewal.

I observe my mind now, the openness of its inner space, and I notice how clear and uncluttered it has become. Within the still room that lies within, I take some time to appreciate the serenity and the emptiness. The silence. I can feel how my mind is recharging, too.

With every moment spent observing my inner world in this way, my body rests more, becomes more dormant, more still. And my mind becomes clearer, more focused, more awake. I sit back, giving myself as long as I wish to enjoy this quiet time, these moments of deep peace. Right now, as I offer myself this space for regeneration to happen, I watch both my body and mind returning to wholeness and health.

## Slowing My Breath, Settling My Body

Have you ever noticed how the speed and depth of your breathing correlate to how relaxed you are? When we're at peace, our breathing is naturally slow and deep. When we're tense, it's short and sharp.

Let's use this phenomenon to our advantage as we consciously slow down our breath, lulling ourselves into a calm state.

⌒

I bring my attention to my breath, to the steady inflow and outflow of air. I notice that the smoother and slower my breathing is, the more relaxed I feel. And so, in order to slow it down even more, I count to five on each inhalation, to five on each exhalation. As I do so, my breathing extends, becoming slower, steadier, longer. Inhaling deeply, I draw breath into the lowest regions of my stomach. Exhaling fully, I empty my stomach of all air.

I repeat this cycle, slowly breathing in for five, deep into my belly, and slowly breathing out for five, emptying my belly. Consciously breathing in, consciously breathing out. I now extend the length of each successive in- and out-breath, counting to six, then seven, then eight. I make my breathing slower, fuller, longer. While doing this, I observe my body falling deeper and deeper into relaxation. With every succeeding breath, my body becomes more and more settled. And still I extend the length of each breath—slow, conscious breathing—and enjoy the peace that follows.

I challenge myself to see how long I can extend each breath for, to see just how deeply, how slowly I can breathe, to see just how fully my body can settle. Breathing in... breathing out... and into that pool of peace I flow. I enjoy every moment, every breath, just letting myself slip into that world of contentment and calm.

## Breathing Myself into Bliss

"Breath is life" is an expression we often hear, especially in yoga circles. While our body certainly would die without breath, what the expression really refers to is something more subtle. By focusing on the flow of air into and out of our body, we bring ourselves into the present in a very natural way. We become more mindful, more awake, thus breathing "life" into this moment.

What's more, when we enter this state of *presence*, the simple act of breathing can become so pleasurable that it borders on nourishment, satisfying us entirely.

———

I draw a slow, deep breath in through my nose, taking that breath down into the depths of my stomach. Now, very gently, I release it. I repeat this simple action, this time with full awareness. Slowly drawing breath in, I watch my breath flowing down my air passages into my body, before exhaling it back up through my air passages and out.

After several repetitions—a deep, slow breath in, and a gentle, long breath out—I notice a change in my body taking place. A satisfied, relaxed feeling has surfaced within, and I take a moment to enjoy the simple pleasure of my body feeling good. As I'm appreciating this inner comfort, I notice how the fuzzy feeling of well-being is spreading itself even deeper and wider within. With each intake and release of breath, warm contentment melts across my chest and into my arms and legs.

Now, as I follow my inhalation down through my windpipe, I observe it as it enters my core, as it merges with the deepest recesses of my body. I watch as my breath comes into contact with a particular part of my body—maybe my hands or legs—and feel an instant surfacing of energy there, a sprouting of life. Now exhaling, gently yet deliberately pushing air out through my mouth, I focus on the feeling of my body settling more, falling deeper into stillness.

I repeat this process, inhaling through my nose and increasing the life force in a specific part of my body, then exhaling through my mouth, deepening my relaxation. This time, as I breathe in, I feel the breath to be something more than air—somehow more substantial and fulfilling, almost nutritious. As I breathe in, I feel the richness of its contents filling me, nourishing me, satisfying me. And as I release it, I relax more. I repeat this as often as I wish, simply focusing on inhaling substance-rich breath, on bringing my body into a higher energy state, then on exhaling and releasing tension, on moving further and deeper into peace.

I notice that this sensation of energized peace now fills my entire being, a buzz of comfort having spread across all parts of my body. I feel I could just sit here forever, enjoying this natural act of breathing, of taking in and releasing air. I am here, entirely present, entirely at peace. I need nothing more. This simple act of breathing in and breathing out, of filling up and letting go, satisfies me completely. I rest here, enjoying the warm feeling of peace that has settled within.

## Setting My Mind Free

We all know how energizing a ten-minute power nap can be, both physically and mentally. During those few moments when we disappear into the mysterious world of sleep, we detach ourselves entirely from our busy lives. On waking, we feel—almost magically—renewed.

How is it that a mere ten-minute rest can have such a profound effect on us? It's because during that brief nap, we are *genuinely* resting. Our muscles are loose, and our breathing is slow and deep. And yes, we are detached from it all.

Sounds a bit like meditation, doesn't it? Indeed, it is! In meditation, we consciously release physical and mental tension and step back from it all, giving ourselves a chance to regain perspective. And just like that power nap, we emerge with renewed vigor.

So, step one in meditation is relaxing our body, enabling the second step: calming our mind. The multitude of body relaxation meditations out there emphasizes how important a stress-free body is in achieving mental calm. By allowing our body to become deeply settled, we can let go of physical limitations as we journey into the unseen avenues of our mind. In here, within the vast, open space of our mind, devoid of boundaries, we have the freedom to explore our deepest, most creative self.

Let's slow down, relax, and breathe. Let's go *deep* within.

⌒

I take a moment to focus on my breathing. As I inhale through my nose, I follow my breath inward, letting it take me on a journey through my body. It guides me down through my chest, all the way into my legs. I simply flow alongside my breath, letting it carry me inward.

Now, as I exhale slowly and purposefully through pursed lips, I follow my breath as it rises out of my legs, upward through my core, and out through my mouth. With the exhalation, I feel my body settling comfortably into the chair I am seated in. I repeat this breathing cycle, simply keeping my focus on my breath, making it gentle and calm, watching it flow in, and out. Again, I follow my in-breath through my nose and into the farthest reaches of my body, into my toes, into my fingers. And I breathe out.

With each in-breath, I feel myself drawing energy into my body. And with each out-breath, I feel myself releasing tension. Inhaling, bringing the energy in. Exhaling, releasing the tension. I am energizing my body with each inhalation, stilling my body with each exhalation. I am becoming brighter and more settled. Inhaling, my body recharging, becoming full. Exhaling, my body sinking comfortably, becoming relaxed. I breathe in, and rich energy enters my toes, filling all the spaces. I breathe out, and tension leaves my toes before washing out of my body.

I take a moment to observe my toes, noticing how relaxed they are. I feel a warm tingle, too—a distinct whir of energy in each toe. And now, from my toes, I move progressively up my body, breathing into and out of each area. I inhale into my feet and exhale out of them, leaving them relaxed. Into my legs I go, breathing into them and out of them, leaving them settled. Into my buttocks, stomach, chest, arms, back, and neck. Each part is left in a state of comfort, of stillness. My whole body is relaxed.

And now, as I take another slow, deep breath, I direct its oxygenated flow into my head. Fresh, rejuvenating energy enters my mind, brightening my inner world in an instant. And as I release the air, my head is left feeling clear and rested, my eyes heavy and relaxed. I do a quick survey of my body as a whole now, and I realize how settled and silent it is, how comfortable it feels. Indeed, a kind of dormancy has crept over my entire body. All that moves, all that is awake, is a spark of energy behind my eyes. A conscious spark—indeed, the bright energy of my mind. And this energy, now fully awakened, is free to express its beauty. *My* beauty.

I notice that this inner spark I feel, the very energy of my consciousness, inhabits a vast expanse within. And it's in the center of this expanse where I find myself floating. I can create anything here, be anything, feel anything. I think of something beautiful I want to be—maybe an angel of bliss, a star of purity, a weightless balloon, or a powerful fire. I visualize it on the canvas of my mind, and I simply allow the experience to happen.

I allow myself to become my vision. Here, within this sacred space of open consciousness, I am free to experience my highest potential. I can become whatever I want in a second. And I do exactly that—I step into my highest self. I step into the enlightened me. And I truly feel that enlightenment, with all its maturity and calm. Here, seated at the center of my conscious, creative mind, I free myself into the powerful phenomenon that is me.

## Emerging the Silent Lake Within

Guided meditations, like those found in this book, are nothing more than inner dialogues geared toward emerging specific feelings and experiences. For example,

"I sense a welling up of peace in my heart." We could then elaborate by adding, "And that peace emerges like a still lake within."

What we're doing is calling upon that very powerful yet underutilized tool in our meditation armory: visualization. By seeing an image in our mind—and we're talking about *seeing* it, in all its four-dimensional, tactile magnificence—we invoke powerful associations that surface as feelings. For some, thinking about a lake may manifest peace and stillness in their heart; for others, freedom and openness might emerge.

Think of and see that still lake. Observe your inner world. What do *you* feel stirring within?

To illustrate the power of visualization, let's imagine you're faced with a challenging situation that requires a quick shot of confidence. You take a deep breath and say to yourself,

"I look within and see a majestic lion, his mane wafting in the wind. I watch as he opens his mouth wide, letting out a roar that rocks my entire body."

If you were feeling a touch timid before, I bet you aren't anymore!

Let's leave those untamed energies of the wild for now and return to the tranquility of our lake. Let's paint that beautiful body of water onto the canvas of our mind and watch as its soft atmosphere filters magically into our hearts.

———

I sit quietly and breathe myself into a calm state. I now visualize myself seated on the bank of a vast lake. As I look out over its waters, I observe how still its surface is. So motionless is the lake that I could almost believe it's made of wax. But as I shift my eyes to just in front of me, to the water's edge, I notice tiny waves lapping against the shore. I take a moment to enjoy the sound of these waves, their slish-slosh as water pushes in, then pulls back. Such a gentle sound—so consistent, so rich.

The fullness of this simple yet profoundly relaxing sound washes through me, soothing me from within. I now hear birdcalls, too, somewhere up above, and I imagine the view they must have of the lake down below. How majestic it must look from high up in the air. I hear another sound coming from behind me—the rustle of wind in the trees— and I now feel a gentle breeze brushing my face. Ah, this cool, fresh air; so rejuvenating.

I take a deep breath in and feel that coolness entering my body, my being. As I exhale, a smile emerges from within. How beautiful this moment is, just being in nature and absorbing her calm energy. Such simple pleasures, yet so deeply satisfying. I cast my eyes to the far side of the lake now, and I see a series of green hills, each one densely forested. I wonder about the abundance of life occupying those forests, about the cacophony of insect and animal sounds. That's another world existing right there in that forest.

I bring my attention back to the lapping water in front of me and stretch out both legs, dipping my bare feet in. The coolness of the water seeps into my legs, bringing another wave of freshness in. I observe the little wavelets splashing up against my feet, sending their energy into me, and I feel instantly connected to nature. With my feet resting in the water, I take it all in: the great lake that lies magnificently in front of me, the forested hills in the distance, the breeze caressing my skin, the bird sounds, and the cool water tickling my ankles.

I sense a deep peace embedded in this masterpiece of living art, a masterpiece I am seated right in the center of. I soak up the spaciousness of it all. And I let go into it, freeing myself into its openness. Now, as I look within, I see that same vastness of my surrounds reflected inside me. I feel a similar openness in my heart. Here, within, I have let go entirely, and all that remains is simple, clean space. The beauty of the lake is inside me—its vast openness, its calm waters, the coolness of its breeze. My inner being is rested and relaxed, my heart entirely at peace.

I sit here for as long as I wish, enjoying the tranquility and stillness that exist around me and within me.

## Expanding My Inner Light

What is the first quality you think of when you visualize light? For many of us, clarity and cleanliness come to mind, as well as warmth—which is exactly the quality we will be focusing on in the following meditation. We'll look into the light and let it lull us into a warmth-inducing experience, comforting our spirit and settling our mind.

⌒

I visualize a golden light, small but bright, at the center of my heart. I observe how peacefully it floats within, surrounded by soft darkness. The contrast between the light and dark is so complete, highlighting even more the light's deep, golden hue.

As I look into this light within, doing nothing more than appreciating its rich color, I notice its shimmer, a misty aura encircling it and extending into its dark surrounds. And within this aura, I sense a distinct warmth. The more I look into the light and its glow, the stronger I feel this warmth rising from the center of my heart and extending outward. I feel my heart coming to life as this radiance fills more and more of my inner world.

As I peer into the ever-expanding, ever-intensifying light, its waves of warmth start spilling out into my body, spreading its comforting influence through me. And still this light, located so centrally in my heart, extends its golden arc. Silently, the warmth continues swelling outward, filling more of me as it melts into my shoulders, down my arms, across my stomach, and through my legs. This river of light unfurls itself across all parts of my body, leaving a feeling of deep comfort, of relaxation, in its wake. My every muscle is perfectly settled, free of all tension.

I look within and see a world of warm, soothing light sweeping through my entire body. It feels so good, this enchanted light and its reassuring glow, warming me from within and making my whole body glow. I let go to the light, allowing it to relax me more and more. I give myself permission to fall beautifully into the fullness of my inner light.

# Chapter 2
# Abundance

Abundance has become a buzzword in recent times, and for good reason. But what exactly is this thing called abundance? How do we go about finding it, and when we do find it, what does it feel like?

Many of us go through periods when we feel there's a certain emptiness to life. In response, we look for novelty and meaning to fill the void, picking up a new hobby, entering a new relationship, changing jobs, or relocating. What we're really doing is searching for that satisfying feeling of abundance that sprouts naturally from new, meaningful experiences, leaving us content and full.

Ironically, rather than abundance being found in the material world—which is where consumerism has taught us to look—it comes from within. Nonetheless, it's certainly true that when we bite into that juicy orange or move into a new house, our life feels abundant and full—but it's all too temporary. Real abundance comes by directing our focus inward and tapping into the depth of our own spiritual beauty. It comes when we gaze into our warm hearts and set our original energy free. Our very essence starts to flow, and it's precisely in that flow where we encounter abundance.

The sparks that activate abundance are all there inside us: the stillness of peace, the vigor of happiness, the magic of love. By taking time to look inward, we shine a spotlight on our virtues and give them license to emerge and spill over into our lives. It's then when we begin to experience that fullness of being called abundance.

## Awakening My Virtues Within

Deep within, we possess all the qualities we could ever wish for. We have—even if only momentarily—experienced probably every virtue imaginable. Bliss, love, courage, determination, patience, peace … we know what these words mean and feel like, because we've been there.

Although these feelings are often triggered by outside events—an adorable puppy warming our heart—they undeniably surface from within ourselves, meaning *we* create them. Not the puppy, as gorgeously cute as she may be. In fact, we're not so much creating these feelings as emerging them. And the implication of this? They exist right now within us—we simply need to recognize them and give them the space to breathe.

With our powerful minds at our disposal to help access that world of beauty within, we should surely be inviting more peace, happiness, and love into our lives. And we can. In fact, with a little effort, we can even become somewhat self-sufficient islands, relying on no one but ourselves to invoke precisely the feel-good experience we wish for. Now *that's* something to strive toward!

Let's reach into the world of virtues within and reawaken our dormant beauty.

———

As I sit here, enjoying the silence of the moment and the stillness of now, I realize that I am like a fertile island within, filled with abundance and warmth. In my heart, I possess every beautiful quality I could ever wish for.

My heart is wise in that way, and deeper than I could ever imagine. I need to just look within and acknowledge the presence of that beauty. And so I cast my gaze inward, into the depths of my heart, and the first quality I see is peace. An entire world of it lies before me, a vast pool of tranquility, eager to express and spread its beauty. And I let it do that. I let it awaken fully and expand its soothing energy throughout my being, extending its feel-good atmosphere across my inner plains.

Ah, peace … how good it feels, unfurled so liberally within, touching the deepest parts of me with its rich influence. And peace is but one of the many qualities existing within me. I see love lying before me, and happiness, purity, power, patience, determination, and courage. These are all housed safely within my heart, like hidden fruits ready to be tasted on a whim. I need to just glance into my boundless inner world, acknowledge the quality I wish to feel, and set it free.

And I do that, by looking within and seeing contentment. I see it shining beautifully inside me, and I set it free. And immediately the energy of contentment rises from within, and it flows. I release myself into its flow, into its fullness, into its truth, and I am swept away in its rejuvenating current.

I take a moment to think of another quality I'd like to experience—maybe love, happiness, strength, or purity. I choose my quality, and this time I see it as a jewel within, glowing brightly. I see its color. I feel its warmth. And I let its radiance swell outward. Within this glow, within the warmth of this glow, I feel the very essence of my chosen quality. I feel the love, the purity, the strength. I watch as the light from this jewel fills more of me. I feel it shining brighter and wider. This quality lives inside me like a flame, dancing and alive. It's an integral part of me, existing right here at the center of my consciousness, at the center of my heart. Deeply embedded in my spirit, in my being, it beams out, making its powerful presence felt to me.

I glow with its vitality, with the richness of its living light, and observe as its radiance spills out onto my skin. My entire body shimmers with its energy, and the shimmer feels so good, so full. In this moment, the glow of this quality is all I know. I am satiated, top to bottom, with its light and the essence within its light.

As this quality spreads out from me, I release myself into it. I let go into its rich atmosphere, and its light washes over me, swims through me, swallows me. I surrender to its abundance, to its vastness, to its vibrance. And in this beautifully saturated state, in this moment of spiritual fullness, I shower my surrounds with a profusion of my very own feel-good light.

## Asking the Right Questions, Finding Truth

Many people—especially those of us with a spiritual bent—spend a fair amount of time looking for answers in life. Yet sometimes it's more the *questions* we ask—with questions being the catalysts for finding the truth we are after—that bring the greatest rewards. Once prompted via a question, our subconscious gets to work, processing its vast information and experiential database to come up with an answer—sometimes when we least expect it!

Let's ask some questions—questions of *relevance* and *depth*—and see what comes to light.

I look within and ask myself, "How am I feeling right now?"

By inquiring into the state of my inner being and listening for the response, I find my gaze being drawn naturally inward. And my energy, quick to follow my gaze, takes me to a place deep inside my body. Here, settled beneath my skin, I take a moment to get a sense of how I am feeling. I now ask myself another question:

"What is the condition of my inner world?"

Again, I listen for the answer. In an instant, I am observing all that is happening down here in this open, private world of mine. Again, I ask,

"What is the condition of my inner world?"

I look around and see very clearly the state of my inner being. I get a sense of how healthy, how whole it feels. Resting here, I observe and experience my flow of life within, as well as the quality of energy within that flow. I ask another question:

"Am I in harmony with myself?"

I pause and listen for as long as is required to hear and feel the response.

"Am I at one with myself?" I listen. "Is my inner energy flowing freely? Is the life I feel inside me in a state of balance?"

I sit quietly and observe the depths of my inner world, allowing answers to surface in their own time and in their own way. All I am doing is inquiring, then patiently listening for a feeling, an experience to naturally surface, revealing the answer. As I ask these questions, I begin to notice a change happening within—a shift in my energy and its flow. And this shift defaults, always, to a state of positivity and growth. That is the magic of my inner world, the beauty of the heart. Its glow is inherently uplifting.

In response to my questions, I feel a blossoming of a healthy inner world. I feel harmony emerging within, a balancing of energy, an inner flow that is even and smooth. I feel a shift toward deeper peace as my energy spreads itself across all parts of my being. Yes, everything is in balance within.

My meaningful questions have led to the most meaningful answer: that of an experience steering me toward wholeness and growth. And through this experience, I learn more about my inner world: its current state, how it functions, what it needs. I learn how to correct imbalances and bring my state of being back into harmony with the true me. And now, feeling full, I choose to ask other questions, too, each one elicited with gentleness and love.

"Am I taking care of myself right now?" I listen for the response, just let it fill me.

"Is this moment beautiful?"

It's through questions like these—about my unseen inner world—that my heart's wisdom is awakened and I am led to truth. I am taken into meaning and into the abundance of being. And as I continue with my day, I continue to look inward, checking on my internal condition whenever I have a second to spare. I inquire with the patience of a student wishing to learn, with the mindset of a spiritual seeker wishing to grow. In this way, I remain connected to the deepest parts of my being and am constantly reminded of the wisdom and fullness within. I listen with love to my inner world, and every second spent listening brings with it another second of growth.

## Exploring the Expanse of My Universe Within

When we talk about the mind, what is it we are referring to? Can we define *mind*? Is it part of the brain or the soul? Does it have physical dimensions, or is it an unlimited, unseen world within— something that cannot be boxed?

Many visualization exercises begin with the likes of, "In your mind's eye, visualize [a quiet, calm lake]."

Where do *you* go to find that lake? Wherever it is, let's go there now. Let's find this place called "mind" and get a sense of what lies within its maze of corridors and chambers.

I look inward to my world within and see that all is calm here. I observe this stillness for a moment, feeling the warm influence it exerts on all parts of my being. I wish to understand this calm more, to go deeper into its substance. For this, I turn my gaze toward my mind. I look into the space that lies within the depths of my thinking world.

In an instant, I find myself at the center of my consciousness, nestled inside my mind. Before me lies a vast expanse, an open space with seemingly no walls, no boundaries. I'm immediately overcome by a sense of freedom, by a feeling of being a child again, able to roam as far and wide as I wish with no restrictions. I head off in one direction within this immensity of my mind, abandoning all physical limitations as I do so. Here, I am free to wander, and I will never get lost. I will always remain at the center of my being. And that center, as I plainly see, is a space that is endlessly large.

How fascinating my inner world is! As I drift about within, roaming without restraint, I discover that, yes, my inner space really does extend outward in all directions. It is boundless, infinite space with nothing to limit my movements. I have my very own universe within, one that rolls out into distant, unexplored territories. And these territories are all part of me. They all exist within the world of my mind. This is the place for real adventure, I realize, right here within me.

I take some time to enjoy the enormity of my inner landscape, feeling myself spreading out into its vastness, of simply letting go into its expanse. And with the letting go comes a feeling of unburdening as I release myself into the endless plains surrounding me. Here, I can extend myself as widely as I wish. I can gaze into my unlimited universe with nothing blocking me or my vision. I have complete freedom. My inner world is without limitation, and I take this time to appreciate the spaciousness, the stillness, the depth of my very own universe within.

## Being Ever-Ready, Stable, and Strong

Sometimes, when that natural burst of happiness, peace, or strength sprouts up in us, it feels like we're surrounded by a protective bubble, shielding us from negative influence. Nothing and no one can pierce our good spirits as we go about our day.

Unfortunately, this emotional armor appears and disappears with alarming regularity. And when it does fade or vanish entirely, the first thing we need to do is *recognize* its absence. A question we might start with to help recognize our encroaching vulnerability is this:

"Could I keep my cool if I were emotionally confronted right now? Would I remain stable in the presence of conflict?"

If the answer is no, then we need to go about consciously restoring our protective shield, enabling us to remain strong in the midst of life's inevitable obstacles. And how do we restore it? By asking that very question above! Amazingly, this simple inquiry into the condition of our stability will already have initiated the process of rebuilding our strength and reemerging our fullness of being.

Let's ensure we're ready for the unexpected by going within and fortifying our spiritual armor.

———

I allow my body to relax, and I go within. Feeling a world of calm down here, I take my attention to the surface of my skin and feel a glow of warmth covering my body. It is spread across me like a sheath, a second skin, encasing me with its substance and warmth. I may sense a particular color in its warmth—a red shimmer, perhaps, or a blue, white, or green one. And within this shimmer on my skin, I sense a gentle buzz. It's like there's a slow, soothing Om sounding within this pocket of warmth encasing me. *Ommm.* I feel an inherent strength in its vibration, a constancy that I know will always emerge victorious over negativity. Such is the strength of my Om. Such is its power and abundance.

As this Om rings out across the surface of my body, I focus on the protective force within this sheath's vibration. I feel its vivid color. I take a moment to appreciate its reassuring strength by simply sitting quietly here within my body, beneath my skin, and observing this hum of sound, this casing of color surrounding me. Beneath my second skin and its warm, protective Om, all is perfectly calm. I am safe. I take these precious moments with myself to enjoy the solitude and tranquility down here, to enjoy the feeling of security and serenity. Now, as I take a conscious breath in, I inhale the essence of the vibration surrounding me, absorbing its color and substance into the depth of my being. I soak up the strength in the Om, pulling its vigor into the very core of my being.

As I breathe out, I breathe power into this energy field that surrounds me, reinforcing it even further. I repeat this, breathing the might of my protective layer in, deep into my being, then breathing out my strength, solidifying and expanding this protective field of energy. How good it feels, seated here within this surrounding force field, secure in who I am. I am grounded, stable, strong. I know that when I move forward into today, I will carry this warm vibration, this field of glowing energy with me.

Wearing my shield of light, I now return to my outward journey, retaining my unique vantage point within. From here, the world is an inviting place, and I look forward to the beauty and intricacies of life.

## Returning to the Magic of Now

We've all experienced the beauty of being entirely present and watching on in wonder as our rather ordinary world transforms into something very special. Simple breathing feels so good, nature comes to life, and people's eyes glisten. This is the power of living in the present, the power of being awake, now. Yet how often do we find ourselves removed from this present? We drift to the past, either nostalgically reliving old memories or trying to wish the unpleasant ones away. The future, too, demands our attention, luring us into concerns about things that probably will never unfold.

Knowing the only moment that exists *is* right now, you'd think we'd spend more time in it!

The expression *presence of mind*—as in, "I had the presence of mind to confirm the details with Sue. And thank goodness I did!"—sums up what we're taking about rather nicely; in order to appropriately respond to any situation, we need to be entirely here and now, fully aware of what's happening within and around us. We need to be, indeed, *present*.

The following meditation brings us back to that present. To *this* present. That's what we need to do throughout the day—remind ourselves of the importance of this very moment and appreciate the beauty inherent in being alive, right now.

Breathing calmly, I take a few moments to consider what it is to be alive, what it is to be conscious of this very moment in time. I become acutely aware of the fact that I am sitting here, feeling the weight of my body in this chair, attentive to the gravitational pull drawing me downward.

I look beyond me now to life as it exists around me: the sounds, the colors, the movement. A dynamic flow of energy exists in my immediate surrounds. I can touch it with my mind, feel it, interact with it. It's alive, just like me.

Now, bringing my focus back to myself, I look inward, locating the sensation of life within me. I take a moment to get a sense of my inner energy, and I feel it surfacing as a distinct vibration within. This simple sensation makes me realize how fortunate I am to have this gift of conscious life.

I am here, and I know I am here. I am having a full-blown experience of life as it exists in me and around me.

This simple awareness of existing in the midst of my animated surrounds, feeling the force of life within, is so profound, so significant. In this moment, there is nowhere else I'd rather be. Right here, right now, being in this body, being in this world, is perfect. It's enough to satisfy me entirely, so replete is it with depth and meaning. I want and need nothing more than this moment, this feeling of being alive, this consciousness of me existing here. I take a moment to appreciate the energy of life as it flows through me, vibrating within. It is so real, so tangible, this inner life force. This is my energy, and how wonderful it feels. This thing called life is truly a miracle. Life exists inside me. Life exists outside me. I am separate from what is happening around me, but we exist together.

I feel my inner flow of energy, and I feel the array of energies flowing around me, outside. My energy and those of my environment exist in harmony, touching and influencing one another. These rivers of energy and their intermingling create the experience of this mystery called life. I realize how easy it is to be satisfied with the simplicity of being present, of seeing life with all its textures, all its layers. Being here, in this moment, I feel complete. This space in time is perfect. I need nothing more. I have everything. I am alive, and this moment is truly beautiful.

## Reawakening My Inner Child

Life can be pretty serious business, and in the sobriety of it all, it's easy to neglect our playful side. Ironically, spirituality—in itself a serious pursuit—brings lightness to our being, and when we're feeling light, playfulness comes naturally.

In the following exercise, we allow the light of our very own soul to guide us down a joyful, childlike path.

———

Sitting quietly, I remind myself to take life a little more lightly. I needn't be so serious all the time. Life is here to be enjoyed, after all. And in order to experience that feeling of lightness right now, I allow my inner sparkle to appear. I watch in wonder as that star of energy at the very center of my being makes its presence known to me, as it rises from the depths within.

Immediately I feel its warmth, its bright energy seeping into and touching all parts of me. It's an energy so pure in its innocence, so vigorous in its radiance, so positive in its glow. The more I focus on my light, on this inner star, the brighter it shines. It exudes a childlike joy, its sparkle like a dance within. I spend a few moments simply watching this energy bubbling to life at the heart of my being, watching as it gains vitality, as it burns more brightly, as it dances more enthusiastically. And its joyful dance reminds me that I, too, am playful and light, like a child. I, too, am free.

By taking moments out of my busy day and connect-ing with my inner radiance, I am reminding myself of my childlike side. I can dance from within, spreading pure light and happy spirit. As I move forward in life, I can engage this vibrant inner light whenever I wish, bringing it to the surface and expressing its exuberance. The simple act of looking within reawakens the light's shimmer, and I feel that shimmer throughout my being. Its radiance expresses itself naturally through my actions as I give myself license to shine.

While living life, I can do my own internal dance simply by gazing inward and finding my star, feeling my light. In this way, I can celebrate the simple joy of being alive. The light within is my inner child—always glowing, always positive, always bursting with life.

Right now, as I become once again conscious of the world around me, I hold my inner light at the forefront of my consciousness. Smiling inwardly, filled with playful curiosity and flowing with warmth, I am ready to explore my adventure-filled life.

## Embracing the Wonder Within

Are you getting your regular fix of wonderful? Look inside … it's there, that iridescent, vital energy that says, "Ah, this all feels fantastic!"

If you suspect you're not feeling perfectly wonderful, you might ask yourself if there is anything actually *preventing* you from feeling good, right now. Probably not, right?

"I feel amazing." Say that to yourself. Now repeat it, slowly. "I feel *amazing*. Oh yes, *this* moment is good."

Let's look deeper at this feeling called wonderful and surround ourselves with its effervescence.

———

I take a moment to think about what *wonderful* means to me. I look within and ask myself, "Am I feeling wonderful right now?" Maybe just by entering the serenity of my inner world and asking this simple question, I already get a sense of something stirring inside: a small, tingling sensation of wonderful. It may be a mere inkling, but it's there.

I take a slow, deep breath, and release. *Ah*, that feels good. I breathe in again, holding it for five seconds, and as I breathe out slowly, counting to five, I let my body drift toward that feeling of wonderful. I do it again: breathing in, holding for five, releasing for five as I relax into feeling good, as I float into wonderful.

Now, as I peer into my inner world, I identify that space within where I feel the most wonderful. It could be in my feet, or in my stomach, or in my heart. It could be in my eyes, or in my smile, or even in my entire body. Wherever it is, I move my consciousness to that place filled with goodness and take a moment to rest there, just being still and present. Just feeling this space, feeling myself in this space, in touch with the feeling of wonderful pervading this space. And I watch as this feel-good energy begins to grow, rising steadily within, filling more of me with its warmth.

I return to my breath and slowly inhale into this very epicenter of wonderful. I notice how its pocket of warmth fires up with renewed energy. And as I exhale, the feeling expands, flowing into other areas of my body, filling me with its essence. Breathing in, into this space, breathing out, and watching as this feeling of wonderful expands. Its comforting influence has spread through vast areas of my body now, its glow deep in my arms, legs, and torso.

I turn to the inner open space of my mind and notice how the warmth of wonderful has seeped in there, too. Indeed, my entire being—body and mind—is enveloped with a glow that feels so good, so full, so wonderful. Sitting here within, I embrace the happy, healing shimmer that fills my being. And the more I embrace it, the more it grows; the more it fills me, the higher it takes me. Resting within, breathing calmly, I give myself over to the goodness that is this feeling called wonderful.

## Connecting to My Inner Flow

Energy, although often invisible, is something that infiltrates every aspect of our lives. Beside natural energy (like that of the sun), and machine-made energy (like the electromagnetic radiation of microwaves), there is our energy, too—both physical and spiritual. This energy flowing within exists as a kind of dynamic charge, always there and—if we choose to look inside—always detectable.

Our physical energy includes the firing of nerve impulses and the countless metabolic reactions happening within us so seamlessly that they're nothing short of a miracle. Then there's the *real* miracle: our spiritual energy, such as our chi, as well as that subtlest of energy emitted by the deepest part of our being, the soul.

Making the effort to observe our own energy benefits us by first bringing us promptly back to the present as we wondrously watch our life forces at work. It also develops in us a deeper understanding and appreciation of this mysterious phenomenon called life.

Let's listen to our own flow of life as we touch the *I* within.

———

Sitting quietly, I become aware of the fact that I am a conscious being. I am here, in this moment, experiencing life. I can see, hear, smell, and taste. And I can feel. I feel the chair beneath me. I feel my feet in contact with the ground. And when I look within, into my inner being, I feel something akin to an electric charge flowing through my body. It's as though my body is wired with a kind of free-flowing circuitry, facilitating the movement of energy to all corners of my body.

I observe this energy flow as its warmth travels to all the working parts of my body. Up and down it goes, left and right. I follow it, just flowing along with this river of inner energy as it moves between and connects different parts of my body. Taking a moment to enjoy the vitality within this current of energy circulating so smoothly, so vibrantly, through me, I sense its nurturing quality as it awakens the different areas of my body it passes through.

For these few moments, I simply sit back and observe my very own electric charge moving through me, nourishing and energizing the entirety of my body. And now, I choose to influence this electric charge. To do so, I pick any positive quality—such as joy, peace, love, strength, or purity—and write that word across the surface of my mind. I see its large letters in front of me, glowing with a specific color. Embedded in that color is the very quality the letters spell out. If the word I see is *joy*, then I allow each letter to be saturated with joy. Joy seeps out, funneling into my being, into my electric circuit within, into that river of energy that moves so freely through my body. I notice how this electricity has taken on a fresh hue now, a new vibration, reflecting this quality emerging from my mind. It flows through my torso, down my arms and legs, and up into my head, carrying the spirit of my quality with it. My entire body is filled with the color of its light, with its richness, with its essence.

I take a few moments to appreciate the stream of energy coursing through me, to enjoy its revitalizing flow. When I am ready, I experiment with a different quality—happiness, or power, or peace—and watch as this quality embeds itself within the flow, producing its own unique, beautiful charge of electricity within. Tuned in to my inner charge of electricity, I move with it, surrendering to its healing vibration. I release myself into the fullness of the flow within.

## Self-Maintenance 101

If we were constantly content and fulfilled, we'd probably not feel the need to meditate. Unfortunately, effortless enlightenment is a rare find these days! As a result, we indulge in practices like self-reflection to identify and correct our imbalances and move closer to the beautiful *I* we aspire to.

There are times when, despite our good intentions, moving forward and upward becomes a struggle. It's then when focused self-reflection becomes all the more important. Simply pausing and paying attention to our internal environment can go a long way toward bringing perspective and clarity to the moment, allowing us to find that optimal way forward while soothing the dis-ease within.

An easy way to get us reflecting on our internal environment is to ask, "What do I need right now?" This inward inquiry—this attention to our needs—prompts an automatic repositioning of our awareness, away from the outside world and squarely onto our world within. In doing so, we're able to assess our current state, and initiate an appropriate response. This simple question—"What do I need right now?"—followed by some attentive listening to our heart's response inevitably results in a positive quality surfacing and filling the void. This is self-maintenance 101—practical, simple, and essential.

If you have doubts, try it for yourself, and watch as that very feeling you're in need of sprouts wondrously to life within.

—————

I take a few slow, deep breaths, relaxing my body, calming my mind. I look inward and ask myself,

"What do I need right now? What do I feel is lacking within?"

I wait patiently for the response. And as I wait, I may sense a flicker of something filtering through.

"What would I like to experience in this moment?"

A specific feeling may emerge. It may be peace I sense trickling through from within, or love, stillness, or strength. It could also be that nothing surfaces initially. That, too, is fine. Either way, I sit back, simply observing my inner world. Again, I ask,

"What do I need right now?"

As I do so, I notice something else coming to life within … a tiny glow, rising from the center of my being. I acknowledge the presence of this inner light, giving it my full attention, and I watch as it grows, as it becomes warmer and brighter. I ask this light, in a gentle yet determined way, to fill me with what I need. Sitting quietly, I gaze deeply into this light within. I open myself up to its divine guidance and listen for its response.

I observe as a feeling begins to surface from within the light. And as the light flows outward, across the interior of my being, I detect precisely the quality I need in its flow. All I'm doing is listening to the light, tuning in to its flow, and watching and feeling its energy seep out into me. I am an open vessel, and my openness allows this energy, this light, to flow. I am setting it free so that I can receive what I need from within. That very quality I was lacking spreads through me, filling all my empty spaces. And the longer I sit here, listening to and observing the rise of this energy within, the fuller I become with the warmth of this quality. Just resting here, observing my world within, I am being filled from the inside by my reservoir of light. A sensation of moving toward wholeness fills me, and it all feels so naturally good.

## Sharing My Silent Shimmer

On a hot summer's day, one can literally see heatwaves shimmering off the surfaces of inanimate objects. But what about us? Do we, too, have our own special shimmer?

Indeed we do—only ours isn't merely heat energy; it's *life* energy.

Let's dive within and find the source of that shimmer. And once we find it, let's inflate and brighten it for the benefit of both us and the world.

———

I turn my vision inward and become aware of the life force within, of that spark that tells me I am alive. This life force—my heart, my soul, my consciousness—has a special energy of its own. I give myself time to locate this energy, to pinpoint the life that exists at the core of my being. Just the simple act of directing my attention inward will reveal this energy to me, this vibration that tells me I am alive. And indeed, I find it. It's here, right at the center of my being.

I take a few moments to observe it, to feel its subtle pulse, its vital energy. As I familiarize myself with my very own living force in this way, I begin to notice how it surfaces from a specific point and flows outward from there, moving into and through my body in waves of calming energy. I observe the effect this energy has on the different parts of my body it passes through. I appreciate how this current moves across the entire span of my body, touching all areas with its vibration. I focus on my skin now and feel a faint tingling sensation as this energy rises to the surface. I become aware of a soft web of electricity covering my entire body, revealing itself perhaps as a tingling warmth or even coolness on my skin. I may even sense a color-field enveloping me, or a particular glow.

In whatever way my inner energy manifests itself on the surface of my body, I simply observe it. I notice its temperature, its color, its vibration. And now, I go deeper into it. What quality exists within its glow? Is it a powerful shimmer? A peaceful glow? A pure radiance? What do I feel within this energy emerging from my core, now spread so smoothly and liberally over the surface of my skin? As I open myself up for answers, I remain seated at the center of my being, at the very point this energy is emerging out of. From here, I can enjoy the totality of this experience of life as it unfolds across my body, across my being.

I now become aware that this energy's glow and the feeling embedded in its glow are expanding beyond me, outward. I free myself into this feeling and watch as it slowly but steadily permeates my surrounds. I consciously nudge this feeling farther afield, increasing its glow, its influence, its power, allowing my positive vibration to alter the atmosphere around me. This requires no effort, just a simple awareness of my energy, then letting it go, letting it be, letting it flow.

As I do this, I feel both myself and my surrounds being transformed, becoming fuller, brighter, more beautiful. Through my positive intention and the brilliance of my energy, I become an instrument for making the world a better place. All I need to do is let my own living energy first fill me with its light and then flow into my surrounds. I set it free, touching the world with my warm spiritual glow.

## Doubling Up My Dose of Energy

The spiritual energy we carry within, although unseen and subtle, is rich with potential. To tap into its power, though, we need to remind ourselves of its presence. If not, we quickly forget all about its potency and, before we know it, it becomes a largely unutilized, wasted resource.

Yet when we do go in search of our spiritual substance—and that search need be nothing more than shifting our awareness inward—we get to experiment with and access its power. As we bring our spiritual energy to the surface, we get a real taste of its capacity to transform the moment as well as us.

In the following meditation, we tap into the energies keeping us breathing, moving, and thinking—indeed, *being*. We reveal their power as we explore the magic that is running through us, right now.

⁓

Seated comfortably, I feel a distinct spark of energy behind my eyes. Its vibration is soft and constant, its gentle pulse lulling me into a peaceful state. Bathing in its glow, I recognize this energy as my spiritual energy, the soul. This energy is me. I am the one resting here, behind my eyes, giving off this soothing vibration. The thinking, conscious being that is me is seated at the center of this spark, spreading my own warmth, my own peace.

I now transfer my awareness to my hands and open my palms upward. I feel a mild pressure in the center of each palm and sense the energy that lies there. As I focus on these pressure points on each hand, on their warm vibration, I notice the feeling becoming stronger. Just being aware of their energy is enough to increase their intensity, their power. It feels like each palm has a little flame dancing in its center—such is this vital force. I realize the healing potential that lies at my disposal here, and I wish to use this energy. And so I do just that. I turn my palms to face the world and set this energy free.

Immediately, I feel warmth streaming out from both palms and spreading into my surrounds. This energy feels unlimited, so rich and constant is its flow. I now turn my palms to face each other only to find they are like two opposing magnets, each palm's energy pressing against the other's force. I play with this energy, moving my palms slowly closer and farther away from each other, appreciating their energies as they squash into one another, then stretch apart.

I now raise my hands slowly upward and turn them toward my face. Without my palms actually touching my face, I maneuver them in small circles in the vicinity of my cheeks. Already I can feel their comforting heat brushing my skin. I detect a distinct healing substance contained within their energy, and I absorb this energy through my face. I feel its goodness entering me, its therapeutic warmth spreading inward. Inhaling, I breathe this energy deeply into me.

I now start to circle my palms gently around my temples, again not making physical contact with my skin, giving myself an energy massage. My temples respond immediately to this vibrant warmth, soaking up its glow. I move my palms to the area of my eyes now, allowing them to take in my palms' soft energy. Instantly I feel my eyes relax as they fill up with the restoring inward flow, as they open up to the vigor and newness within the energy.

Now, moving my palms in front of my forehead, I feel another distinct energy just behind my forehead. It's the very energy I felt earlier behind my eyes: the energy of the soul. Again, it feels as though two opposing magnets are being brought together—a play of energy between the soul pushing out its radiance and the energy emerging from my hands.

As I experience these two unique energies, I let them merge. I let their warmth melt into each other. I become aware of their meeting point: two dazzling energies dissolving into one another. As I slowly move my hands back and forth, toward my forehead and away from my forehead, I feel that stretching and squashing of energies. Both are so pure, so powerful, so tangible. These energies are my life force, my clean inner world being projected outward.

Finally, when I am ready to come back into the consciousness of my surrounds, I lower my palms, keeping them open and preserving the dancing flames of energy above each one. And behind my eyes, that unmistakable sparkle of the soul still shines brightly. Feeling equipped to continue with my day, I take these energies with me. I know of their power and their potential in leading me toward health and fulfillment.

## Giving Thanks

Making conscious effort to be grateful for what we have is a useful tool in learning to appreciate the moment and bring contentment into our life. We may live in a comfortable house, or be blessed with excellent health, or have a particular talent, but if we neglect to remind ourselves of our good fortune, we can quickly become complacent, taking these gifts for granted. Before we know it, insatiable hunger seeps in as we try to fill our lives with more *stuff*, with more quick fixes in our pursuit of stimulation and fulfilment.

Let's be thankful for being here, right now, and appreciate the simple things in life.

Sitting here, I become aware of the chair beneath me, of how my body molds so perfectly into its contours. How comfortable I am, just releasing myself into its softness, just letting my body sink down. Thank you, chair, for giving me this support, for letting my body rest in you. I take my attention to my breathing now, my slow inhalations, my gentle exhalations. How soothing this simple activity is, just bringing air in and energizing my body with its freshness, then releasing that air along with any tension. Thank you, breath, for allowing me to become more conscious, more at peace, more focused through observing your smooth flow into and out of my body.

I focus on the room I am in now, on its interior, and pick out an object that gives me joy. I reflect on how it brings me that joy. I think of the role it plays in making my life happier and easier. And I thank it for this. I now think of someone special in my life and about the support they give me. I thank them, with feeling, for being in my world, for being the uplifting influence that they are.

As I give thanks to the many aspects of my life I am grateful for, as I choose to see and appreciate this beauty and fullness around me, I feel my heart opening wide. I am truly grateful for this life in which I have been blessed with so much. My reality is unquestionably good and filled with abundance.

## Chapter 3
# Heart

In meditation, when we look within to the deepest part of our being, we venture into our spiritual core. And that simple inward glance into those untold depths awakens our heart, allowing it to touch us with its wisdom and beauty.

Let's explore those very depths, finding out for ourselves the heart's potential in filling this moment with meaning and truth.

## Leading from the Heart

Sometimes we perform actions—especially the mundane ones— with a heart that's neither activated nor involved. We switch over to an almost robotic mode for those habitual chores "not requiring heart"; after all, brushing teeth and submitting tax returns are just things that need to get done!

But there *are* times when more meaning, more substance, could have resulted had we called our heart into action. Take, for example, a simple goodbye; we can conduct it with heart—or without. Contrast mumbling a hurried goodbye to your mother with one said from the heart, *with* heart—and with all the inherent love, power, and feeling infused in a heartfelt expression. How very different would these two goodbyes be in both impact and meaning.

What we're talking about is opening up our inner being and allowing our pure energy to surface and flow. We're talking about being natural and honest in our expression. And the easiest way to ensure honest expression is simply by—you guessed it!—putting more heart into it.

So how do we do this? We simply place our heart at the forefront of our being—*before* engaging in an activity. It's a conscious repositioning of our feeling center as we intentionally grant our heart permission to lead us with its wisdom. And then we follow its energy.

What we're doing is exposing our heart to the world and putting full trust in its substance, in its guidance and expression. And the result? An ensuing action that is a beautiful "living from the heart." An expression that is natural and unconditionally true. The heart, after all, knows nothing *but* truth.

When we bring our hearts out into the open while living life— be it while washing the dishes, taking a walk, or spending time with others—our simplest actions are transformed into something powerful. They immediately become filled with purpose and meaning, and we feel fulfilled.

Let's conduct a simple exercise in bringing our feeling center to the fore as we move with the heart and watch as beauty surfaces.

⌒

Before I conduct my next action—be it a simple one, like eating, walking, or doing a household chore; or a more

complex one, like talking to a friend or confronting someone regarding a sensitive matter—I tell myself,

"I will conduct this action from the heart, with the
heart. I will bravely put my heart out there and allow it to
lead me."

To begin this repositioning of my heart, I move to where
it is within. I go to that inner space from where my feelings
emerge, to the emotional center of my being. I can feel my
heart very clearly here as a field of warmth and purity. And
I notice how it wants release. I feel its potential, its power—
and its wish to express that power. So, I give it release. I open
up my heart and let its light flow, let its essence gush outward
as it reveals its full, blooming beauty. I let my heart's vitality
fill my consciousness, brightening my vision in an instant.
This dazzling, explosive energy is the lens through which I
see and experience the world.

And now, with a radiant mind and a flowing heart posi-
tioned at the forefront of my being, my outlook is filled
with depth and truth. Everything I see is illuminated,
empowered. Yes, this is my heart in operation, influencing
every part of my world in an inspiring way. This strength
I feel is the potency of my heart, beaming out and influencing who I am. It determines how I feel, how I conduct
myself. And its outpouring is powerful. I have awakened my
heart's energy. Its warm, lively presence invigorates me. By
being in touch with my heart, I realize I am unstoppable.

Now, to invite that experience of conducting myself
with heart, I relinquish the reins, giving myself over entirely
to the wisdom and vigor of my heart. In giving full release

to my heart's clean, fresh energy, I allow its beauty to provide the spark, the impetus for my next action. As I perform the action, I release my heart's essence into it, observing how it fuels and guides my action—and watch in wonder as the action is replete with feeling and sincerity.

With my heart open and out there, meaning permeates my movements, my words. My actions are fulfilling and powerful. Everything I do in the presence of my heart takes me forward toward beauty. By keeping my heart at the forefront of my being and letting its energy guide me forward, I bring value and joy into the present, into my actions, into life.

## Adventuring Inward in Search of Love

No single word has been spoken, written, or dreamed about more than—you guessed it—love. Ironically, despite all the attention it gets, love is arguably the one key element *lacking* in our world today. Maybe what's needed is a love revolution where we go beyond musing over love, instead bringing it unabashedly to the surface in all its glory for all to see and share in!

But what exactly is this magical phenomenon called love? Is it a physical sensation, or does it emanate from a deeper emotional or spiritual place within? What does it feel like to truly love and to be in love?

What we do know is that love makes us feel good...so good that we can't stop speaking, writing, and dreaming about it!

In meditation, when we're fortunate enough to stumble into that inner enchanted bubble of spiritual love, we quickly realize how unlimited it is in nature. So all-encompassing is its vibration that, as it radiates through and beyond us, we recognize our potential to touch not only those in our immediate surrounds with its sparkle, but those in faraway places, too.

Ah, so much to contemplate when it comes to love! Best we get to work, then, in uncovering the mysteries embedded within its gentle yet powerful embrace.

———

I relax my entire body, allowing it to become still. In the quietness that ensues, I look within and let myself become empty. Here beneath my skin, all is silent, undisturbed. A space of inner peace exists around me. I am a hollow vessel, open and ready to be filled with all that is positive and good.

I take a moment to reflect on love—on what it is, on what it feels like. If I were to experience love right now, what sensation would emerge? I focus on my heart now, on that deep, calm space within. It, too, is open, ready and receptive. And I give it what it wants: light. I simply pour molten light into my heart, watching as it streams in. I can feel this light, too, filling up my heart-space. I can feel its purity, its strength. And within this light, within its beauty, I feel something else, too: a sacred warmth that is unmistakably the sensation of love.

I notice how this love is giving off a special vibration, one that fills my heart. It is a comforting energy, glowing gently within, brightening up the core of my being. This loving light feels so good, so natural, so real. It exists as a spiritual substance in me. And as love circulates within my heart, I let its radiance extend outward, releasing it into the deep crevices of my body. Soothing waves of warm energy emerge from my heart, flowing out and massaging my entire body with their soft vibration. I feel them healing me with their purity, with their warmth. And as more and more of me is filled with light, I feel how my heart, too, is growing, expanding outward with the light. My heart-space is now extended across my entire body. I am composed of heart and its light-filled love alone. My inner radiance fills all corners of my body as warmth filters out and melts into every part of me.

I look within and notice with wonder that my being, in its entirety, is bursting with vibrant light. Now, as I look even deeper within to the very cells of my body, I see and feel love's pulse filling them, too. All these tiny physical building blocks of my body are charged with love's vibration. Every cell overflows with love's glow, and the energy spills over into me in a river of love.

I now direct this stream of inner light toward my mind and immediately feel the refreshing effect this radiance has on my consciousness, bringing instant clarity and bliss. As pure light streams in, I feel my mind begin to expand, growing wider and wider until I see before me a vast, bright landscape. All is resplendent within. My consciousness and its love-filled light extend into the farthest reaches of our world. I touch distant places of our planet with my light. I let this light flow out and into every being. I shower the world with love, letting it touch and uplift the hearts of others. Right now, I can give, because I am full. To give is natural and easy. I have one voice, and this voice is love. I exist within the beauty of clean, inspiring love.

## Announcing My Heart to the World

Adverts grab our attention with their sharp, succinct messages. T-shirts, too, occasionally have a catchy line emblazoned across their chest, some of which really resonate with us. There are those that are attractive in their simplicity, like the one I recently saw: "Ride!" printed under a drawing of a bicycle. Plain, but impactful. Other slogans are humorous in nature. "I speak fluent sarcasm" was one that tickled me. And, of course, there are those that are thought-provoking and inspiring, like my forever favorite, "A world without strangers."

Wouldn't it be wonderful if we all had a positive slogan written across our shirts for the world to draw meaning and inspiration from? Well, in a way, we can. But instead of buying a printed T-shirt, we'd wear an invisible inner slogan written across our hearts. We would carry subtle messages within, expressing things like "Love is alive!" or "I'm touching the light right now. Can you feel it, too?" What's more, by bearing these messages, we'd naturally be transformed into the embodiment of that message.

All it takes to become these beacons of light, these messengers of inspiration that the world is so in need of, is regularly asking ourselves the following simple question:

"What single quality would benefit my surrounds right now?"

That question alone taps into our spiritual intelligence as we learn to assess the state of our external environment, alongside our capacity to summon a virtue from within and offer its beauty outward, moving our surrounds to a higher state.

Let's ask that very question now and listen for our heart's response.

————

I sit quietly and observe my surrounds. I get a general sense of the atmosphere here before asking,

"What single quality would benefit my surrounds right now?"

I go within and listen, opening myself up to any whisperings of a response. What message does my heart have for me and for the world right now? What quality, what kind of energy, is my heart yearning to share? My heart, after all, is that wise, spiritual space, and it knows what's needed in this moment. What's needed is that I bring my heart out into the open, enabling its wisdom to surface. As I listen, I start to feel that very quality blossoming inside. It may be love, peace, purity, or strength. Whatever it is, this is what my heart wants to offer the world.

Now, with this virtue rising inside me, I think of an appropriate one-line message expressing the virtue. It may be something simple, like, "Love shines brightly," "Peace is my purpose," "My heart sparkles like a diamond, touching all," "I am strong, as are you," or "Touch my light; it shines for you." I sit quietly, repeating this message. As I do so, the essence of the message fills my heart, and I feel myself being transformed by its quality. Its energy flows through my entire being before overflowing outward into the world.

Radiating with this feeling, I take a moment to reflect on the message's core virtue, be it love, peace, purity, or strength, and I see that word alone spelled out in bright letters across my heart. *Love.* I see those four letters glowing within, and inside that glow is a tangible feeling of love. *Peace.* The letters shine with tranquility. *Serenity.* All is calm.

This feeling drifts through me, a palpable vibration, before flowing outward. And as this energy moves through me and out of me, I can enjoy its presence, its richness, its positive influence. I can go deeper into it, too—deeper into the feeling, deeper into understanding it.

I think back to my original one-line message, and I offer it again in its totality to my surrounds. In imparting it to the world, I am transformed, very naturally, into a messenger for spreading its fragrance. I have become the embodiment of its core virtue as the energy of this quality circulates through me and out of me in a stream of living light. I offer this message, imbued with spirit and heart, to our world, creating a positive shift in the atmosphere for all to draw healing and help from.

## Surrendering to the Guidance of My Heart

While our physical heart pumps blood through our body, our spiritual heart pumps a deeper, subtler life force through our being. But what exactly *is* the spiritual heart?

It's often considered the space from which feelings and emotions emerge, as opposed to the head, our center of logic. It's that place deep within, holding an energy we can summon in an instant to bring light into our life. It is that inner space from which truth, warmth, and love emerge, a space imbued with wisdom that, when we place our trust in it, leads us in the right direction.

Let's summon our heart's guidance. Let's trust it implicitly and watch as our journey through life fills with profundity and wisdom, every step of the way.

———

I go within, into my spiritual heart, and settle myself comfortably in its pocket of warmth. It's a deep, safe place, offering solitude and peace. I simply rest here, observing the stillness and serenity existing within my very own inner space. This is my private retreat center, a sacred place I can dive into at any time to recharge within its cocoon of silence and calm.

For now, all I do is rest here, quietly reenergizing myself, allowing myself to become full once again. I give myself over to my heart and let it fulfill its rejuvenating function. It is, after all, a space replete with healing potential. All that's needed is me entering it and very consciously being here, feeling its warmth as I open myself up to that health-giving energy. Seated here within my healing center, I am giving myself the time and space to become whole again. I am simply resting in silence, doing nothing, just being. As I let my heart work its magic on me, I allow myself to feel this sensation of returning to fullness, of becoming complete again.

When I am ready, I gently return to the surface and become aware once again of the outside world. I come out feeling renewed and clear about who I am. And with this clarity of vision, I am somehow more resilient to life's challenges. I can navigate through today with a deep wisdom, emerging from having touched my heart. And I shall remain connected to that inner spiritual space, feeling its warmth, its perfect energy emanating from that place of silence within. Yes, I can still feel its strong yet gentle power.

I allow my heart's energy to keep resonating through me as I go about my day, expressing itself as it showers light into my activity and onto those I come into contact with. I bring my heart and its radiance to the surface, into my actions, into my interactions. I put my heart out there, trusting it completely. And I follow it. I follow its wisdom and energy, letting its strong, warm influence lead me. I offer its guiding light to myself and to the world, knowing its contents are true, and pure, and always beautiful.

## Revealing the Treasure Chest of My Heart

Imagine if our heart were a treasure chest filled with jewels, each jewel bursting with the vibration of a specific virtue. Whenever we wished, we could simply reach in and pluck out one such jewel … maybe a red ruby of love, or a purple amethyst of contentment, or a sparkling diamond of purity. By bringing it to the surface, we'd be doused in its beauty while very naturally sprinkling our surrounds with its fragrance. Our heart's contents would be on full display, offering their pure substance to the world while constantly reminding ourselves of our own innate beauty.

What follows is precisely such an experiment where we emerge virtues—*jewels*—from the depths of our heart and offer them to the world.

I visualize a large treasure chest filled with sparkling jewels. Each one glows with a different color and appears to have a life force, a unique vibration. I now imagine my heart to be this very treasure chest full of these beautiful, bright jewels. I feel them shining at the center of my being and know that I am free to bring their energy to the surface at any time.

I now choose one that catches my eye and pluck it out, holding it in the center of my palm. I gaze in wonder at its glowing energy, this magic stone that shines with some deep inner force. I observe its color and size. It may be a big red oval or a small blue sphere. I wonder what quality it holds within, what virtue is embedded inside its colorful light. As I take some time to appreciate its vibration and color, it starts to reveal its quality—perhaps as a cleansing green, or a powerful red, or a calming blue, or a nourishing purple. And the more I focus on this jewel, the stronger its cleansing—or powerful, or calm, or nourishing—energy becomes.

I now place this jewel back into the treasure chest of my heart, and my heart immediately opens up with the jewel's fragrance and glows with its vibration. And the more my heart glows, the stronger and wider the feeling spreads, seeping into my body now. Before I know it, my entire being is awash with this beauty emerging from my heart-space, waves of vibrant health rolling outward. As I release this vibration beyond the confines of my body, as I shower my surrounds with its light, I simply give. Because giving is natural and easy from a space as rich as my heart, from a fountain overflowing with light. As this energy moves through me and out of me, I feel its fullness firsthand. I experience the essence of its beauty, its purity.

Now, looking within, I once again see that array of jewels shining in my heart. In an instant, I feel a rush of the sum total of their power rising in unison, and a flood of pure light engulfs me. These are jewels that shine eternally with their determined, inspiring light. I am in touch with my heart, surrendered to its radiance, its flow, its ever-present light that lifts me as well as those around me.

## Unlocking My Heart

Living with an open heart is considered, certainly in spiritual circles, as something that encourages self-development and a deeper understanding of both ourselves and the world around us. This act of looking within and consciously opening our hearts as we go about our day can also transform our actions from something ordinary into something extraordinary, perhaps even sacred.

But what exactly does it entail, this opening up? What does it *feel* like when we perform an action with a heart that is wide open? What kind of energy flows into our movement?

Let's rummage for answers in the realm of experience as we harness that power and beauty within. Let's open our hearts and saturate this moment with life.

⎯⎯⎯

I visualize my spiritual heart, that space at the very center of my being from which feelings originate. Indeed, this is the space from which *I* originate. I take a moment to consider the quality of the light that might surface from such a sacred space, on the purity of the energy that would surely emanate from my spiritual core. Looking closer at my inner world, I notice a little door occupying the entrance to my heart. It is locked, but glancing down, I see a key in the palm of my hand. I place the key in the door of my heart and unlock it.

As I gradually open it, just a crack at first, a beam of crystal light streams out from within, brightening my surrounds. I observe this light and notice how perfectly clean it is. Marveling at its simple beauty, I sense a distinct depth and power housed within its radiance, a wisdom of sorts. I wonder about the potential energy lying in wait within my heart, ready to be released should I open the door wide.

Wanting to explore what's there, wishing to fill myself with this very energy, with my heart's enigmatic light, and wanting to let loose its full power, I push the door wide open. In an instant, I am flooded by a torrent of exquisite spiritual light. Energy gushes from the depths of my heart and washes over me. I feel the rush of its power and purity coursing through my body, through my being. Thousands of warm prickles of energy move into the deepest parts of me, cleaning me, lifting me, empowering me. As I feel myself growing, transforming, becoming full with the outflow of energy from my heart, I allow the light to flow to the surface of my being and to beam outward in a beautiful arc of luminescence.

I become aware of a specific quality embedded within this arc of light—perhaps peace, or love, or strength. I feel that very quality in the light as it streams out from my heart, effortlessly washing through me and out of me into the world. As it does so, it cleanses me with its purity, and it cleanses my surrounds. What a gift this spiritual radiance is, flowing straight from my heart. What a gift it is to me as it refreshes and uplifts me. What a gift it is to the world as it inspires those who are touched by its splendor.

Now, as I step back into my day, into the physical world, I leave the door to my heart wide open. I move forward, rooted deeply in the power and beauty of my inner world. My heart is bright and full, and I am overflowing with spiritual light.

# Chapter 4
# *Transformation*

"You can achieve anything you set your mind to—just believe in yourself!" How often we've heard these words from educators, family, and friends. And it's true; a big part of becoming success-ful—however we may define success—has to do with positive thinking patterns and an inner dialogue that inspires self-belief.

Do you constantly encourage yourself with loving words, or are you prone to criticizing yourself, berating yourself for every mistake you make? Do you start your day celebrating abundance, or bemoaning the things you think you lack?

By harnessing the power of the mind—be it through posi-tive thinking, visualization, meditation, or simply an enthusiastic approach to life—we can move toward being the best version of ourselves. By being intentional—*positively* intentional—we can harness the energy of transformation.

## Opening the Gates to Transformation
The physical world contains a myriad of symbols we can use to our advantage while growing the human spirit. Think, for example, of

a lion. What comes to mind? Strength, for sure—so much so that when we manifest this mighty creature in our heart, an equally mighty version of ourselves emerges. When we think of the ocean, qualities of purity, fullness, or openness may come to mind. The mountains bring stability, while fire offers power. Indeed, we could make an endless list of things in our environment alongside the related virtues they give rise to in us.

In the following meditation, we draw on this very power of association. We'll be using a gate as a symbol of transition; by passing through it, we will automatically move from a negative or neutral state to a higher, more empowered state. This "gate" can be anything from the space between two trees or poles, to a real-life door we walk through. The gate, of course, represents a passing from the old to the new, from the mundane to the extraordinary. As we transcend this barrier and come out the other side, we do so with renewed vision, allowing us to continue our journey, inspired and fresh—heck, maybe even enlightened!

———

Walking slowly and consciously, I see what appears to be a gate up ahead. But this is no ordinary gate. It's a transition zone replete with potential for personal transformation. I realize that by moving through it, I will pass from my current, relatively ordinary state into a higher, wiser, more enlightened state. I will exit the other side of this gate— indeed, this portal—with a fresh, powerful perspective on life. And so, observing the gate up ahead, I approach it very slowly, very respectfully, very mindfully. I am mindful of the change that will take place as I traverse it, as I pass through from this side into what lies beyond. I ready myself for the inevitable transformation that awaits me at the crossing point. I prepare myself for the simmering energy within the gate's domain.

Moving closer, I already feel traces of its electric atmosphere. As I continue to approach the gate, this energy becomes stronger, more palpable. I am now a mere step away from the transition zone, full of anticipation of what awaits me. And now, very consciously, I take that final step, and into the gateway I go.

A burst of power envelops me from every direction—from above, from below, from both sides—shooting through my being. It is a power that cleans, that lifts and awakens. And within this surge of life charging through me, I sense a capacity for inducing wholesale change. I can harness this energy, right now, and use its power for personal transformation. This is the potency of the force at my disposal. I need to simply apply it in an accurate way. I need to just *let* it clean me, lift me, awaken me. And I do so.

As the energy gushes through me, I let it rock my being in the most powerful, life-changing way. I let it destroy all that is negative, obliterate the unwanted, purify my every fragment of being. I let it fire up all that is positive in me, giving life to my beauty, my wisdom, my clarity.

Now, as I take another step and move beyond the gate, I sense the wonder of this transformation having taken place within. I feel the great change that has happened in me. It's as though I have passed out of a dark tunnel and stepped

into the light. My consciousness is bright and inspired. I am
ready for anything. This is the new me, the highest me.

Exiting the gate, all is beautiful and exciting. I move forward with a foundation of self-belief and spiritual strength.
I walk with intention, my gait filled by light, my vision
bursting with positivity and passion for life.

## Reveling in the Soundtrack of My Mind

If we were to spend an entire day wearing headphones, listening
to our favorite songs, and someone directed a nasty comment our
way, we wouldn't hear it, let alone react to it, right? We'd saunter
straight on, blissfully unaware of their negative intention, caught
up only in the beauty of our music.

Let's allow that beautiful soundtrack to flow through us. Only
instead of music, we'll create another kind of soundtrack: one
composed entirely of encouraging, empowering words, ensuring
we walk through life bursting with positivity and light.

———

As I move through the day, I experiment with a range of
inspiring, simple thoughts:

"My inner world is calm and quiet."

I say these words to myself slowly and with conviction.
"My inner world is calm and quiet." Having said them with
feeling and with love, I now stand back, giving the words
time to exert their warm influence. I give them the time
and space to roll around within and work their magic on
me. And I watch as the result of these words take hold, as
their energy rises in the form of beautiful feelings. I feel

that inner calm, that quiet. It exists within me in a very real way. The energy of the affirmation grows, and my inner world starts to transform with each repetition, said slowly and gently. "My inner world is calm and quiet." The essence of these simple words spreads through me, filling me. I now experiment with another affirmation:

"I walk toward the light."

I allow the imagery of my words to flood my world. Me, coming closer to the light. Me, feeling the light. Me, bathing in the warmth of the light. And finally, me, entering the light. With each repetition, spoken intentionally, I go deeper into the experience. I enjoy this tactile encounter with light firsthand. I truly am experiencing the light. The light is here, and I am in it.

I experiment via other affirmations, and with each one, I patiently allow a visual, sensory experience to follow. Each affirmation starts out as words, then mushrooms into an experience.

"Strength burns like a fire within." I feel that fire. I am that strength.

Each affirmation uplifts me as fully.

"I look into the beautiful space of my heart, and a river of light flows through it." I touch and play with the river of light within.

Each affirmation is unique, bringing its own magic.

"I am at peace with myself, and the world is a special place to be." And from my perspective of peace, my surrounds are friendly and inviting.

"I tread softly on our planet, spreading love." As I walk forward, appreciating life, I gently share my heart with the world.

Each affirmation gives rise to distinct feelings, feelings that grow in me and around me, creating a shield of light. They keep me moving decisively forward. Nothing can shift me off this path of positivity. My words, my feelings, and my experiences keep me grounded in wholeness, in fullness. Within, I flow with the music of my own uplifting thoughts, with my own affirming commentary. This loving inner dialogue ensures my life is saturated with feeling and meaning every step of the way.

## Spring-Cleaning the Room of My Mind

Within the room of our minds, things can get awfully cluttered. Overthinking can create a jumble of what should be our sacred inner space. So what's needed to reemerge our clarity? A spring-cleaning, of course! We need to clear away the clutter and rekindle the quietude of our inner world.

Are you ready to get to work? Great! Let's create that clean inner slate—and with it, a platform for fresh, inspiring thoughts. Let's clear away the dust and give clarity a chance.

———

I imagine my mind as a room within. I now take myself there, stepping into my inner space. Looking around, I see the expanse of this room: its contents, its walls, its windows. I notice that it is somewhat cluttered—certainly not the clean, free-flowing space I'd like it to be. It's a little stale and musty, too, with a distinct haze of dust hanging in the air. Nonetheless, as I glance around, a comfortable feeling of detachment envelops me, a feeling of me being an outsider, simply observing my mind with a degree of objectivity.

This sensation of being somewhat removed from the clutter, of being a casual observer of my inner world, feels good. Simply by examining it in this way, things already appear less messy. I focus on a window on the far side of the room, its curtains neatly drawn. What a difference it would make if I opened those curtains—and the window, too. I move toward it and pull the curtains aside. Immediately, a stream of golden sunlight floods the room of my mind, curling its way in and across the interior, finding every corner with its light.

The effect is one of instant clarity, of brightness within. The light is warm, too, and I take a moment to savor the healthy glow that has settled inside me, to feel its comfort spreading across the expanse of my mind. I am being lulled into calmness as this golden warmth works itself through my inner being. The warmth and the light are certainly good—but I need fresh air, too. So I open the window, and a cool breeze instantly washes deep into my mind.

As it sweeps in, it pushes out the stale air and dust, leaving behind crispness and clarity. This air, so oxygen-rich, is enough to make me giddy with its substance. And as it continues to stream in, touching every nook of my mind, it cleans and reenergizes me. I take a moment to stop and observe the current state of my mind, to feel the warmth, the light, the fresh air. How good this feels! How my spirits have been lifted! Transformation is happening in me, right now, and I can feel it. Golden rays of warm, clean light continue to bathe my mind. Fresh, crisp air flows freely in. I embrace this inner clarity, this calm. I invite it in, more and more, letting it fill me, and fill me more. The warmth comforts me. The light heals me. The air invigorates me. I sit still, doing nothing, just appreciating this inner cleanliness, this inner glow.

As the sunlight and oxygen continue their inward flow, as they soak deeper and deeper into my mind, into my being, I am cleaned more, lifted higher. Now, finally, when I am ready to shift my awareness back to the outside world beyond the room of my mind, I do so gently. As I rise to the surface, I remain conscious of my inner room—of its tranquility, its clarity, its brightness. The outside world seems so much easier to navigate with a mind as clean as mine. And even as I step back into the world, I know I can retreat into my quiet, orderly inner space at any time. I can recharge by taking those few moments to let the warmth, the light, the air back in. Just one step inward is all it takes. I need to simply open the window, after all, and let that stream of light and oxygen in.

## Breaking Old Habits, Bringing in the New

Are we the same person we were yesterday? Or do we become a slightly different version of ourselves every day? Indeed, a more telling question might be this: Are we *content* to be that same person we were yesterday? Or are there aspects of ourselves we'd like to improve on or change?

There probably are habits we'd like to break, or personality traits that could do with a little polishing. Maybe we bite our nails, or smoke, or overeat. Maybe we procrastinate or are easily irritated by less-than-perfect situations. Maybe we lack confidence, or patience, or the ability to relax. Whatever it is, we all have areas in our life that need fine-tuning.

So, how do we move toward becoming that better version of ourselves? One way is to treat every morning as a fresh start, free of yesterday's lingering negativity. Through purposeful reflections and decisive meditations, we can relegate our unwanted habits and character traits to where they belong: the past. The only moment that needs to exist—indeed, that *does* exist—is now. Today, not yesterday, requires our attention.

So, are you the being of yesterday, or today?

Another equally important aspect in personal transformation is reminding ourselves that we are the creators; we can become whatever and whomever we want to be in this moment. This second in time belongs to us; it is our open, empty canvas, and we can create what we want with it. And when we happen to make mistakes on the canvas of the present, that's okay, too. Every second is a new second; one of life's greatest blessings is that we are granted a virtually infinite number of fresh starts in the forever-renewing present. We *can* launch the next moment in our life with a clean mental slate, taking with us the lessons we've learned and those things we hold dear while discarding the unwanted. Our dreams for our future radiant self can be brought forward to the present and realized today. We need to be decisive, though. We need to want it enough to take action now.

Let's do that. Let's initiate action and bring our dreams forward. To now.

———

By listening to my breathing—my slow in-breath through my nose, followed by my gentle out-breath through my mouth—I bring myself into the present. I follow my breath as it flows in through my nostrils, down my windpipe, and into the depths of my stomach. Releasing my breath through my lips, I observe its flow as it exits my body.

I repeat this simple exercise in awareness, inhaling through my nose and out through my mouth. With each successive breath, I become more aware of my body, of how warm and settled it is. I am simply falling into calm, into stillness, into silence.

I observe my mind now, that space inside my head from where I control my thinking, my feeling, my movements. My life. It's in here that I regulate my feelings, my actions, my movements.

Seated inside my mind, inside this control tower deep within, I recognize very clearly that I am the sole creator of my world. I create thoughts, and these thoughts are the energy creating my mood. Thoughts are the building blocks of this moment. They determine what I feel. They determine how I feel about myself. I am the artist, and I can mold my self-image in whichever creative, beautiful way I wish. It's not the outside world that defines who I am.

*I* define who I am, through these very thoughts. Knowing this, I choose to be intentional with my thinking, crafting thoughts that encourage and uplift me. Through decisive, inspiring thinking, I become the person I wish to be. Yes, I am that powerful being, fashioning my present and, in doing so, building a bright future.

To reinforce this, I remind myself that, right now, I carry the spirit of peace and strength within. This is the real me, the current me. I am peaceful. I am strong. And yes, maybe I do have habits from the past I am not proud of. Let me remedy that right now by simply leaving them behind. I think of a bad habit or trait I had and reflect on the last time I acted under its influence. Maybe I got angry too easily, or I let my mood be spoiled by something trivial. Maybe that habit was something tangible, like biting my nails, or smoking, or eating things I know I shouldn't. I remind myself that that was then. And this is now. The time I acted in that way belongs to the past, to a period I have left behind.

I make the firm decision, right now, to remove its influence on me. It is behind me, gone. I commit it to the past, and in doing so, I extinguish any power it had over me. It was, anyway, something I neither wanted nor needed in my life. I am relieved to be rid of it, relieved to know *I* am the one in power, not the habit. I have taken back control. I have complete jurisdiction over my life. The past, and any heaviness it carried with it, is finished. Gone.

This present moment—where I am right now—is a fresh moment filled with beauty and positivity. With peace and contentment. This is what I want, not that. I am strong and have the power to be who I want to be. I am a clean, pure slate, filled with the clarity and newness of the present.

Now, in order to reinforce my personal transformation, my transition to a life fueled by positivity alone, I reflect on a virtue that serves as an antidote to that old habit. If it was anger I suffered from, let me find peace in my heart, right now. If I was lazy in the past, let me counter that with the buzz of enthusiasm. If I was greedy, let me be content.

I let the countervirtue blossom within like a rose in full bloom, spreading its fragrance, its colorful presence through my entire being. I am this. Any lingering negativity is obliterated by this fragrance, by my steely resolve, by my rock-solid determination to be the person I want to be. Any irritation I may have had has been replaced by patience and love, any weakness by strength, any uncertainty by decisiveness. Right now, I emerge these virtues. I bring them into my mind, to the forefront of my being, by telling myself that I am this. I am serenely patient. I am deeply peaceful. I am boldly confident. I am resolutely strong.

I repeat this simple affirmation—"I am this"—and let myself experience the totality of its force within me. This quality vibrates across my being, a living energy coursing through me, touching and transforming every aspect of my existence. Any residual negativity is destroyed by its might. The purity of this quality has entered my biological makeup; it's in my cells. I pulse with it. My body and my mind radiate with it. My spirit bristles with it. I am thoroughly transformed, and I feel that transformation. I feel the new me. And as this quality shines out, strong and pure, it has the power to transform those around me, too. People look to me as a role model of this quality. And as its light surges through me, I observe how other qualities surface alongside it. With patience comes relaxation, stillness, tolerance, and peace. With confidence comes strength, stability, and resourcefulness. The virtues are all connected. By giving myself the time and energy to experience one virtue, I invite a host of other beautiful virtues into my life.

I take a moment to observe these other qualities emerging so naturally in me now, recognizing and acknowledging each one as I experience its essence. And as they surface in me, I make them all an integral part of my present, of my being. They are my antidote to negativity. My inner world is positive and bright, and in the presence of light, darkness and negativity cease to exist. This is the real me, the new me, the me who is decisive and bright.

## Learning Lessons from Life

As we move through life, we encounter a myriad of circumstances. In fact, that's just what life is: a series of experiences strung together into one miraculous symphony. If we consider all we go through in a single day, it's no wonder we're quick at learning to play this game called life!

Every situation offers us an opportunity to learn something new, either about ourselves or about the world around us. And it's especially the challenges—those situations tempting us into reacting impulsively and negatively—that offer us the greatest learning opportunities. If we can step back before reacting and take that deep, centering breath, we're affording ourselves the space to consider our response. In doing so, not only are we tak-ing concrete action toward defying negativity, but we are opening ourselves up to a valuable life lesson, too. This brief prereaction pause allows us to detach ourselves from the situation and gain perspective—with perspective being the first thing we lose by reacting impulsively. The world becomes our real-life, real-time teacher. And what better teacher could we wish for than life itself!

One useful exercise in helping us master our responses to chal-lenges is to proactively *imagine* ourselves in situations we know press our buttons. We visualize ourselves facing that very trial and watch ourselves responding as a spiritually mature person would. In this way, we become well-versed in dealing with difficult situa-tions—albeit only in our mind—and when the real situation does arise, we sail through with flying colors!

⁓

As a vibrant, living being, I become aware of the influence I have on my surrounds. My every thought, feeling, and action creates some form of vibration. I become aware of the activity happening around me, too—of the series of actions and reactions unfolding before my eyes.

By observing myself within this colorful flow of life, I can learn so much about myself and the world. I need just step back, take a few slow, centering breaths, and become the observer. And as I observe, I can reflect on what it all means to me, living here within this forever-changing, dynamic world. How do I respond to the myriad of events unfolding in my surrounds? What can I learn from the challenges I am presented with, challenges that are in fact my opportunity for growth? By responding to them in a mature, spiritual way, I can become experienced in this thing called life.

To initiate this growth process, I imagine one such challenge. Maybe I am on my bicycle as a car roars past, too close for comfort. Or I am in a car and someone neglects to thank me for giving them a gap. Or I greet someone, and they don't greet me back. Or a colleague is rude to me. I choose one uncomfortable situation, and I see it playing out in my mind. I particularly take note of the emotion it gives rise to in me and my response. Do I react in an impulsive, negative way, or in a more considered, mature way, where I simply observe the emotion as it rises in me, then fades? Do I let myself be swallowed whole by the emotion, or do I stand back and recognize it for what it is: a passing wave that comes and goes?

I now replay the situation in my mind, this time seeing myself responding positively. As I sense the flicker of emotion rising in me, I take a deep, centering breath, reminding myself that I am a mature, spiritual being. That I am not this negative emotion bubbling up in me. That this emotion is simply temporary energy passing through me, a wave that, within seconds, will be gone, forgotten. By pausing in this way—one deep breath—and observing the emotion as something external to me, I am reminded of my more enlightened side. I am in control. I come out of the situation victorious, very easily, very naturally, by having stepped back and become an observer of my emotion. I now replay this situation one more time, and as I'm dealing with the challenge, I ask myself,

"What lesson is life offering me right now? What is this person or situation able to teach me?"

It may be that I lack a certain quality, and this situation is the perfect opportunity to practice it. If it's tolerance I'm short on, I might ask myself,

"How would a perfectly tolerant person respond in this situation? What would the thoughts and actions be of a spiritually enlightened, tolerant person?"

And I see myself becoming that angel of tolerance, my actions reflecting that of an enlightened being. I am an example to the world, a teacher of tolerance to those around me. I am the one who has mastered this quality.

It may be that the situation requires stillness or patience, compassion or strength. I allow this moment to be my chance to practice that very virtue. How would an angel of stillness respond in this situation? And by doing so—through my mature response and the experience I gain from acting in this way—I begin to build strong, healthy habits within myself. Having attained victory over this challenge, I now know how to conduct myself in similar situations. I have tasted victory, and victory becomes a habit. It now becomes easier to respond in an enlightened way, every time. And yes, with practice, I can be victorious in all situations. Maybe a long line at the supermarket is offering me the opportunity to practice patience. Let me respond by saying,

"Thank you for this opportunity to practice patience in my busy day. Thank you for giving me a chance to breathe deeply and calmly as I center myself and consider my response. Thank you for giving me this much-needed time to be present, to appreciate the existence of those around me. Thank you for teaching me to become the observer as I stand back and watch superficial emotions waft by."

In this way, every situation allows me to develop into being the person I wish to be. I step into my mature self and act as an enlightened person would, allowing growth to happen as I journey along the varied pathways of life.

## Stepping into Infinite Consciousness

Barriers—both physical and mental—exist everywhere. We know the physical ones well, like the borders separating countries or a bank balance preventing me from buying *that* bicycle.

Mental barriers, though, are more subtle, and often harder to unravel. Maybe we lack the motivation to achieve our goals or the courage to pursue our dreams. It's these unseen barriers that prevent us from uncovering our highest, deepest self. These are the ones hindering us from accessing our true potential as unlimited, spiritual beings.

Mental barriers can be likened to inner blockages preventing our strength and wisdom from flowing freely. Fortunately, with reflection and focus, we can dissolve these blockages in an instant, enabling our hearts and minds to open up once again and blossom with fresh thoughts and feelings. This free-flowing energy allows us to step into higher experiences and our highest self.

Let's dive within, shovels in hand, and clear those pathways leading to our higher self.

———

I look inward, below the surface, and go into that deep, quiet space within. Here, in the vast, untapped world of my inner being, of my mind, I can roam freely. Here, in the world of spirit, things are entirely nonphysical. All that exists is intelligent space, open and unlimited. No walls, no barriers. This is the subtle world of consciousness, of thoughts, of feelings. And here, in this infinite inner space, nothing can hold me back. I am free to wander in any direction as far and as deeply as I wish. I am free to feel without caution. I can experience love, or bliss, or peace, right here, right now. I am free to create without restriction, to build a new, enlightened me. Here, I am free to step into my highest self. All that's required is that I shift my focus inward, as I have done now, into the space of my mind, into that sacred room that is always a mere thought, a mere glance away. Here I can experience true openness, true vastness, true wisdom.

And so, with the conviction that here, within, I have direct access to my highest potential, I allow my mind to expand, to grow beyond the confines of my body. I allow my beauty, my spiritual substance, to spread out into the world around me. I feel this expansion as a broadening of my power and light, as an outward flow of my inner world into the outer world. This spiritual space I inhabit streams outward until it touches the farthest reaches of our planet.

And still it spreads more, into the outer planes of the universe. I allow my being to touch and encompass everything in existence. My consciousness is infinite, extending outward forever. Not a single barrier exists to prevent my growth. Nothing can obstruct me reaching my potential. I am universal consciousness, touching all, embracing all, loving all. I am out there, exploring as deeply and as powerfully as I wish. No experience is beyond me. I am simply consciousness, and consciousness is beyond physicality and its barriers. I am here, and I am everywhere. I am full. I am all-encompassing, conscious power. I have the inherent ability to be whomever and whatever I wish to be.

With this freedom, I choose to reach my highest potential, right now. I choose to step into the highest me and become that self-realized spiritual being of light. I feel the spark of enlightenment inside me. It is bright. It is perfect. It is simply me, being me—unlimited, conscious light.

## Inviting Renewal

Expressions like "Starting with a clean slate," "Every moment is a new moment," and "Live in the now" all convey a feeling of fresh beginnings. They remind us not to fixate on the past or stress too much about the future but to instead create a bountiful, beautiful present. We have, after all, been given that powerful gift of a present that renews itself moment after moment, meaning each day really is somewhat of a clean slate.

One way to invite the awareness of a fresh present into our day is to use specific actions as "rebirth triggers"—be it every time we open our eyes at the start of the day, sit down to meditate, go to the bathroom, eat a meal, or start a new conversation. Before conducting that particular action, we go briefly within, take a centering breath, and become present. Become new. *Feel* ourselves becoming new.

"I will conduct this action as a new me, as a fresh, reawakened version of myself. I will allow clean energy to fuel this action."

This preaction preparation, done consciously and with focus, can be mere seconds in duration. The result? That routine activity—brushing our teeth—will signal a fresh start, and our body and mind will naturally follow suit, inviting newness back in.

Let's take that brief journey within, reconnecting with ourselves as we initiate newness.

I slip inside my body, going deep within. As I sink below the surface, it's as though I have dived into an ocean. There is a vast world down here, stretching out in all directions. Embracing the openness and silence of it all, I take a moment to observe the atmosphere of this space that is my inner world. How dark and cool it is; how tranquil. Resting comfortably here, I am like a baby in the womb, protected and content.

Within this soft, silent world, I am still and at peace. This is my space, a shelter perfectly designed for me to retreat into at any point, to gather energy and recharge myself. I can become new here. Resting here, regaining power in this way, I feel clarity emerging in me. I observe that I am alive, existing right now as a conscious being. And this consciousness allows me to dictate my experience of reality. I can choose who I wish to be. I can step into my highest self. And I do that. I step into a higher, newer state—a fresh, sparkling me.

I observe this feeling of renewal, watching as it burgeons in me, changes me, lifts me. For as long as I wish, I remain in the stillness of my revitalized inner space, appreciating the simplicity, the cleanliness, the wholeness within. By just being mindful that I am here, in this open inner space, I feel growth happening in me. Within this clean slate of my mind, I remind myself that I am a creative being. I can construct precisely the reality *I* wish for. It's me who decides how I feel and who I am. This is my world, and I create the energy and atmosphere here. Right now, my wish is for beauty, and so I emerge beauty. I see the beauty. I feel the beauty. It is in me, and around me.

Finally, when I am ready, I allow myself to slowly emerge from my depths and return to the surface. As I gradually rise, leaving behind the clean space of my inner world, I return to the outside world, feeling energized and bright. It's like I've woken up from a long, nurturing sleep. I have surfaced from that deep space within where I touched the highest me. And having emerged with clarity and positivity, I remain that best version of myself. I have risen as a renewed being, a shining light. I have fresh vision, and the radiance of my light spreads out through me and into the world. I am whole, inspired, and brimming with new energy and clean light.

## Clearing Life's Path with Light

As we move forward in life, obstacles—both big and small—are unavoidable. But let's be honest: a large portion of these obstacles are hardly noteworthy. Minor frustrations, like traffic or slow computers or people who mildly irritate us, form the bulk of our everyday challenges.

Importantly, it's how we *perceive* these challenges that determines the impact they have on us. With a positive attitude, we can reduce—or even nullify—these everyday humps. By staying connected to our inner power, by walking within our own light and shining out our pure intentions as we move through life, we can overcome, and even incinerate, negativity.

———

I feel the sparkle of the soul within, illuminating my heartspace. I let this light grow, and I feel it becoming stronger and bigger, brightening the vastness of my inner environment. I allow it to spill out through my eyes, beams of light shining in whichever direction I turn my vision. Looking ahead, the road before me is brightened by my beams of light. They have the power to sweep away obstacles lying in my path with their purity, with their cleansing force. Illuminated by my very own radiance, the path ahead opens up before me, inviting me forward.

As I head off on my journey, my way forward lit up brightly, I feel confident and carefree. My inner and outer world shine, and within the clarity of my forward-facing light, I have the focus to tackle obstacles with boldness and precision. My powerful vision holds me in a positive state of mind. As I walk forward and encounter challenges, I know I am strong enough, wise enough, intentional enough to emerge victorious. I neutralize obstacles with my vision of light, with the optimism embedded in the light, with my unwavering intention to live a calm, contented, inspired life. I move forward safely and peacefully, protected by my own deep, reassuring light.

## Becoming the Highest, Most Resplendent Me

Would you believe me if I said transformation can happen in two simple steps? One, we have an intentional, encouraging conversation with ourselves. Two, we surrender to and become the essence of those words. We *feel* them, and make them real.

Becoming the best version of ourselves can be—and should be—that easy.

Through loving self-talk where we speak to ourselves in a determined yet caring way, where we observe the fullness of our words taking root in our heart, we can initiate sincere transformation. We can step into being the person we wish to be simply by listening to and feeling—by *becoming*—our words.

Still not convinced? Then let's try it out right now and kick-start the surprisingly uncomplicated process of personal transformation.

—⁀—

I use my breath to bring me into the present, tracking its flow as it enters me. I let it take me to the farthest reaches of my body, following it all the way down to my toes. Now,

I follow it back out as it streams up through my body and exits me. I repeat this exercise, following my breath into my toes, then following it back out of my body. With each breath, I feel myself becoming more and more still. And within this stillness of being, my mind becomes clear, my focus sharp, my senses entirely present. And being awake to the present, I realize this moment is the most important time in existence. Right now, I bring life to my dreams. This moment is my moment, and I choose to spend it lovingly with myself.

I reflect on one quality I wish for—maybe peace, purity, silence, lightness, love, bliss, or strength. And I simply tell myself I am that. "I am peace," or "I am purity," or "I am love." Again, very slowly and with determination: "I am this."

As I repeat it one more time, even more slowly than before, I give myself time to experience it, to go into its depths. I feel the gentle, soothing warmth of the quality rising within as I speak the words. This quality exists here inside me. And the more I see and acknowledge and feel it, the more it grows. I sit here, observing this feeling as it intensifies in me, as it flourishes. And now, I become it. I step into its atmosphere and feel its fullness as it radiates out from my core and surrounds me. I feel it inviting me further into itself with its magnetism, and deeper in I go.

I visualize it emerging as light from my heart now—perhaps golden in color, or blue, or red. It rises out from the center of my being, becoming bigger and brighter. I let this light fill me, and the light's warmth is saturated with my chosen quality. I truly am this. I sit here in stillness, enjoying the light and the vibration within the light. My entire being is suffused with this quality—my every muscle, my every fiber. Transformation is happening within, right now.

I feel my individual cells absorbing this quality, taking on its essence. I am in a state of growth, in a state of becoming that which I wish to be. This quality fills my entire being. Right now, this is me: simple, beautiful light, replete with the richness of my chosen quality. I am transformed and exist as the highest, most resplendent me.

## Removing the Veil of Doubt

Stress, in some form or other, is an everyday part of most of our lives. But in truth, much of our stress comes from worries about the future, those *what-if* worst-case scenarios we indulge in and the energy-sapping anxieties that follow. This bleak outlook is like a veil of pessimism, distracting us from reality and preventing us from *seeing*.

What follows is a meditation where we consciously lift that veil, allowing us instead to look out at the world from a place of positivity, clarity, and abundance.

———

I sit quietly, eyes closed, and listen to my breathing. As I do so, I find myself drawn to a quiet place within. I go there and listen to the soothing silence pervading this inner space. In the clarity of the silence, I realize that my vision can get blocked by concerns about the future, concerns that are often unrealistic. They take me away from the present, preventing me seeing the beauty within this moment.

I visualize these concerns about the future as a veil covering my head, keeping out the light, obstructing the beauty in the present. With my eyes still closed, I imagine the feel of this veil draped over me, the way it tickles my face and blocks my vision. But now is the time to remove the veil, to enable a return to clarity, to full awareness of the present and of my surrounds, to being conscious of the people around me and their inner worlds. To do so, I visualize myself pulling back the veil, ever so slowly, from my head.

As I begin to draw it up, inch by gradual inch, I feel it tickling my chin, my cheeks, my nose. Slowly, as more and more of it is removed, outside light begins to filter in through my closed eyes, and I notice my inner world becoming brighter. Light is coming in—and with the light, lucidity, and the potential for a more conscious, focused way of living.

As more light spills inward and my mind is lit up further, everything seems simpler and clearer. I needn't complicate my world by unnecessarily worrying about the future. What's important is being present, feeling the light, and doing what is necessary to enable a bright future. And now, to summon this state of being present, I tune in to the sounds of my surrounds, noticing how three-dimensional, how alive they are.

I continue to lift the veil, opening up my awareness, clearing my mind. Finally, I remove the last remaining section of the veil from my head. Even though my eyes are still closed, I feel that my inner vision—my consciousness—has been restored. Light streams into my mind, and I am replete with an energy both bright and abundant. I am fully present and eager to explore the world in this open, alive state.

And now, very slowly, I open my eyes and take in the beauty, the colors around me. I look at the world with a fresh, clean perspective. I see everything for what it is: majestic and full. Nature is radiant. People shimmer with depth and color. It's clear to me that a new consciousness has dawned, and I breathe in my world—a world alive with positivity and vigor, with opportunity for growth and personal transformation. I walk forward, excited about the prospect of living life without a veil. In this heightened state, I can truly see, and what I see is beautiful.

## Lighting the Candle Within

A candle, in all its understated simplicity, is a powerful symbol of spirituality. Its form, straight and solid, represents stability and strength, while its flame, warm and bright, shimmers with positivity and hope.

As we reflect on all that a candle symbolizes, let's imbibe its array of empowering qualities.

———

Visualizing a candle, tall and sturdy, I imagine my body to be like that candle. I, too, am strong and stable, my posture upright and balanced. And I feel this strength, this stability, deep in my core.

I now visualize the candle's golden flame and imagine that flame to be my mind, a light shimmering behind my eyes. I feel its bright, warm glow spreading light within. This flame and its powerful, bright energy keep me tall, keep me strong, keep me fueled with positive energy. Within this fire of my mind is a force that allows me to be the person I wish to be. It is a fire that destroys negativity, a purifying furnace. By simply directing this inner flame onto aspects of my personality I'd like to change or be done with, I can incinerate the unwanted in an instant. My inner fire heals and transforms. And I use the power of the flame and the purity of its light to clean me from the inside. Right now, I direct this flame to any negativity within—to the unwanted, to the waste. And I burn it up. I cleanse myself until all that remains inside is beauty and light.

I feel the flame's warmth, its positivity, continuing to glow within. I feel its bright force. And in the presence of my own powerful light, I feel how easy it is to transform myself. I can be whatever I want to be. I exist inside the flame, and it's from here, at the center of this fiery energy I carry within, that I create my reality. Indeed, this dynamic glow is the very essence of me—my distilled, highest self. That sensation of light I feel within, that's my heart, my soul. This warmth I give off is my spiritual substance, my potent energy that burns negativity and creates beauty. I shower this energy, this light, across the interior of my being, destroying the unwanted, the redundant, the old.

I build a bright, fresh, new me. My inner world has been transformed with light.

Now, as I return to the consciousness of my body—that stable, strong instrument—I remain aware of the flame within. I feel the power of my inner world, and its expanse is filled with light.

## Exploring the Corridor of My Mind

When we look within and consider the vastness of this thing called "mind," we may well be left wondering where, if at all, our inner world ends. By observing and experiencing its expanse, it's as though we're stepping into an infinite space—indeed, a world without boundaries.

The *products* of our mind, like our thoughts and imagination, are without limits, too. Our inner world is a fresh canvas where we can paint our dreams, then bring those dreams to life. Whatever quality or experience we wish for, regardless of how magically surreal it may seem, can be manifested within in a second via a single, creative, focused thought.

Let's journey into the incredible faculty of the mind and manifest something truly extraordinary. Let's change our life for the better, for good, right now.

———

I go within and imagine a long, dimly-lit, quiet corridor running through the center of my mind. On either side is a series of doors. Looking closer, I notice that all the doors, although closed, have brightly lit words signposted above them. As I begin to walk slowly down the corridor, I read each sign I pass. Silence, says the first one. The next one reads Love. Then Power, Purity, Peace, Courage, Patience, Lightness, Tolerance, Contentment, Divinity, Bliss, Determination, Truth. Indeed, there is a door for every virtue imaginable.

I take a moment to reflect on which quality I'd like to explore right now and choose the corresponding door. I stand before this door, gazing up at its sign. There, in bright letters, is my chosen virtue. As I focus on the word, on its individual letters lit up so brightly in front of me, I take a moment to anticipate what might lie behind this door. What kind of energy would exist in a room entitled Courage or Bliss, or whichever virtue I've chosen to delve into?

I grasp the door handle and turn it, opening the door just a crack. Immediately, a beam of light washes out over me, and that light—a mere sliver—is suffused with precisely my virtue. I breathe this light in, getting a heady scent of the quality embedded in it. In an instant, I know I want more.

I swing the door open and step in. The room glows with a warm, golden light, rich and full. I sweep my fingers through its radiance and feel its substance, feel the very quality that was signposted above the door. I close the door behind me, wishing to contain its powerful atmosphere. Standing still amid the fullness and vitality of this light, I notice how alive the room is with this quality. Resting here, doing nothing but being present, I feel my skin absorbing this virtue, feel the essence of this quality filtering inward through the surface of my body. As I breathe in, I take in more of its richness, watching as it enters me and seeps into every corner within. This quality is trickling in in its most complete, concentrated form. The longer I stand here, the more I absorb, until I feel like I am melting into the surrounding atmosphere, becoming one with its virtue. Having opened myself up to its richness, having absorbed it into my being, I have become it. I am this quality. It encases me; it is in me. We are inseparable, one.

When I am ready, I take one final breath, inhaling a last serving of its substance before moving toward the exit. And as I step out of the room and back into the corridor, I can still feel the resonance of this quality deep in my core. Gradually reemerging my awareness of the outside world, I leave the corridor of my mind and return to my surrounds. Recharged and brimming with the spirit of this virtue, I feel perfectly equipped to continue my adventure in life.

## Surmounting All Limitations

As human beings, despite being on a constant quest for self-discovery and growth, we nevertheless struggle to achieve our full potential. One possible reason is our tendency toward negative self-talk, which ties into the next reason: holding on to limiting beliefs as to what is possible. Such self-imposed mental barriers act like gates, blocking our flow forward and upward while preventing us from reaching the heights we are deserving of.

There's good news, though. The inherent beauty of a gate is that it can be opened as easily at it can be closed, meaning we can choose to move through it whenever we wish. This barrier is nothing more than a temporary construction of our own creation. And those swaths of fresh pastures and potential we see on the other side are our bounty once we choose to advance through the gate. It's up to us, though, to take that single, intentional step forward and into the beyond.

In the following meditation, we do just that: we fling open our restrictive gates and, in doing so, nullify all our limiting self-beliefs. We free ourselves into the world of opportunity and march toward those dizzying heights destined for the likes of us.

⁓

I am aware that I can be more than I am right now. I can be happier, more peaceful, more loving. I can live a more rewarding, meaningful life. Being here, right now, I recognize this immense potential for growth. However, whether it be through lack of confidence, limiting self-beliefs, or simply not opening myself up to and exploring the vastness of my inner being, I impose false restrictions on myself. These act like a gate, blocking my path forward and inward, preventing me from experiencing the real me. The mature, self-realized me. But this gate is, of course, never locked. It is merely closed—for now. And I was the one who closed it, meaning I can open it. I visualize this very gate up ahead.

As I approach it, I notice I can see through it, and what lies beyond is a large, open field inviting me to come forward and live out my full potential on its green pastures. I notice how attractive that verdant plain is—a world where I can explore the real me, the fulfilled me, the highest me—and it's waiting for me, on the other side of this gate. I walk up to the gate, sensing the freedom that lies beyond. I place both hands on its metal railings, knowing that by opening it, I will release all internal blockages, all self-imposed limitations. And so, with the determined thought that I wish to free myself into the vastness of my potential, into the greatness that is me—that, right now, I wish to be everything I am capable of—I give the gate a firm push. It swings open smoothly, revealing a path leading to that beautiful field, that inviting pasture of opportunity, that world without constraints.

As I step through the gate, I feel a great burden being lifted from me, a sense of having let go of all that held me down. A lightness envelops me, and I feel like I am ascending without effort, simply gliding forward, toward my highest self. Here, in my unburdened state, I can become the me without limitations. I can reach the heights I aspire to. I can touch—and be—who I want to be. And that's what I choose, right now. I choose to be the highest me.

Again, I feel that lightness of spirit within, lifting me. I feel myself rising as the rumble of unlimited potential stirs to life inside me. Here, stimulated by this surge of fresh energy within, I can do anything, feel anything, become anything. Standing on these infinite pastures, I can express my full potential as a creative, self-realized being. It's the real me in operation here—the wise, courageous me. Here, I am unstoppable. I can explore previously unexplored aspects of my being, discovering new talents, new feelings, new wisdom. I can achieve greatness, even enlightenment.

By throwing open those gates and stepping beyond them into the infinite, I have given myself license to discover a higher form of living. I have granted myself access to new ideas, to an expanded intellect. And now, as I walk into this open field filled with freedom and light, I am empowered. Empowered to explore my beauty and express it in its full spectrum of colors. Moving forward in my new world, I feel the promise of fresh consciousness shining brightly within. I ascend with every step taken, knowing every dream I wish for is a mere thought away. My thoughts are that powerful. I think it—and enter it. I become it. All it takes is one second, one thought. I have stepped into the most beautiful and mighty version of myself, and I stride forward, feeling the rousing glow of renewal within.

## Spinning the Virtues to Life

By looking within and inviting silence, we can get a real sense of the depth of our being. Within the silence, those subtle, special aspects of ourselves we aren't always aware of surface, and we uncover a bouquet of virtues. But without the silence—without this regular practice of looking quietly within—our virtues are easily neglected at best or forgotten at worst. Days, even months may pass without a true experience of peace, bliss, or love. By failing to touch our inner beauty on a consistent basis, we forget what lies within, despite the essence of our beauty being a mere inward gaze away. The longer we go without experiencing the magnificence of spirit, the more we think it's normal to *not* be touched by its magic.

When our inner world dims, we need to reignite it. One way to do so is to breathe energy into it, with that energy being the practice of self-reflection. It's when we reflect on some singular aspect of ourselves that our inner focus sharpens, and it's this focus that draws us into silence. In the depths of uncovering one aspect of being, our mind stops its incessant production, instead reverting to a mode of listening and feeling. It's then that an atmosphere of silence materializes in us.

Another way to rekindle the light of our inner world is by talking lovingly to ourselves.

"I look within and see a space that is soft and still. And amid the stillness, I start to see clearly. I see my beauty as it emerges and rises to the surface. It shines. I shine."

This brief inward focus reawakens our dormant virtues. Every one of us has, after all, touched peace at some point in our lives—and probably every other virtue, too. We *know* what peace and love and happiness feel like. We just need to reemerge them by directing our thoughts onto them. This simple reflective process has the power to summon the virtue, nourishing it as it brings it back to full life.

Try asking yourself a simple reflective question involving a virtue. For example,

"What does true peace feel like?"

Wait and listen for the response. It will come, often via a tangible reminder of what that virtue feels like.

In the following meditation, we're going to play a little game to reawaken all the goodness within. We'll randomly pick a letter of the alphabet and think of a virtue starting with that letter. Then, by reflecting briefly on that very virtue, we'll give it the space and energy to rise to the surface and offer us a clear and immediate reminder of its brilliance.

Find your letter, spell out a quality (examples listed below), and take a moment to reflect on it. And *voilà*; your heart will do the rest!

Appreciation, Beauty, Confidence, Determination, Enthusiasm, Friendliness, Gentleness, Helpfulness, Innocence, Joyfulness, Kindness, Love, Mindfulness, Nurturing, Openness, Patience, Quietude, Respect, Spontaneity, Truthfulness, Understanding, Vitality, Well-being, eXuberance, Youthfulness, Zeal.

———

I randomly allow a letter of the alphabet to surface in my mind. If *S* is what pops up, I think of a virtue starting with *S*—serenity—and explore this quality in whichever way I choose. Maybe I see the word *serenity* written across my mind's eye, followed by the sensation of serenity blooming inside me. Or maybe I attribute a color to serenity—a light blue—and feel a wave of rich blue light suffused with serenity emerging in my heart and seeping into my being. Perhaps I imagine what it would be like to experience perfect serenity and then simply drop myself into that experience, let it happen, give myself over to it. Serenity is here within me now. I am this. I needn't think about it—I need to just feel it. Be it. So simple, so natural—and into serenity I flow. *Ah*, so this is what serenity feels like! Or maybe I reflect on what serenity means to me, on what actions would flow from a truly serene heart. And I visualize myself doing just that: acting serenely.

I see myself going about my day, interacting calmly with the world, a serene smile lighting up my face. And so it is that I explore the depths of serenity, experiencing *my* version of it firsthand. And when I am ready, I pick another letter.

*A*—appreciation. I appreciate this moment, this chair on which I am so comfortably seated. I appreciate the warm, healthy glow I feel coming from my body, this glow that is the very vibration of life. I appreciate the fact that I am experiencing this moment, right now, with full awareness and full life.

*E*—enthusiasm. I feel a buzz of excitement within—an energy that tells me I am alive. I am brimming with inquisitiveness, eager to explore my mind and my feelings, eager to explore life.

*M*—magic. I look around, and wherever I cast my eyes, I see beauty. I observe the wonder of life playing itself out around me. I see movement, sounds, and colors—the energy of life in motion. I look within and feel my own life force and realize that, yes, this thing called life truly is magical.

As I continue to pick different letters and new virtues, I give myself license to play with each one's unique beauty. I allow myself to become that innocent, curious child again, enjoying each virtue in its pure and perfect form. I approach each letter and its virtue with a sense of wonder, never quite sure what associations and feelings will emerge. Within me exists a world of virtues, and by unlocking and emerging them in this way, I am deepening the pathways leading to each one, making them more accessible. The more I practice a virtue, the easier I can call upon it whenever I wish.

They become part of my life, constant companions, feel-good additions to my existence. I choose another quality, and there it is: perfect and multifaceted, sparkling within.

## Lifting Off into Lightness

Feeling light—both mentally and physically—brings with it a host of benefits. Not only do we develop a more relaxed attitude, allowing us to find greater enjoyment in life, but our energy levels increase, too. Lightness also implies less internal clutter, enabling clarity of mind and better focus. With focus, we can move toward where we need to be, fast.

Let's invoke this underrated feeling of lightness in our meditation and make it a natural part of our everyday life.

⁓

Sitting quietly, I look within to my inner world, and down into it I go. Here, beneath the surface, I start to get a sense of just how quiet things are, how protected and pure this world inside me is. I now imagine this inner space of my being to be a balloon. With each in-breath, I inflate it, and I feel myself filling with air. I breathe out, then in again, inflating the balloon further. With each successive in-breath, I feel myself becoming fuller, filling myself with more and more lightness—so much lightness that all of a sudden I feel like I'm on the verge of floating upward. I breathe in once again, and this time it happens. My feet push off gently from the ground, and up I go.

Ascending, I take a moment to appreciate the sensation of being surrounded by air alone. A feeling of openness and freedom envelops me. I have been released into the vastness of empty space. I am weightless, suspended in midair with nothing around me. And up and up I go, floating higher and higher.

As I glance down, I see the earth spread out below me in all her beauty. Mountains stand tall in their three-dimensional ruggedness with river-filled ravines winding their way between them. The water of the sea in the distance is a pristine blue, and I notice the intricacy of the coastline with its snaking bays and peninsulas. Up here, so detached from it all, I can truly appreciate the magnificence of our planet—all the greens and browns and blues, all the shapes and contours. Everything looks so peaceful, so divinely inspired. I feel a gentle breeze rocking me left and right, lulling me deeper into comfort.

Every movement up here is so smooth, so effortless, so serene. I am simply flowing with it all, sitting back and surrendering to the breeze, allowing myself to be nudged this way, that way. The weightlessness brings with it a sense of freedom. And wanting more of this freedom, I make the conscious decision to let go even more, to let go of everything, to release all tension, to free myself into the unlimited—into the infinite. As I do so—as I release myself entirely—I feel every burden dissolving within me.

I feel my heart opening up into my surrounds as I start to expand outward. My being, my energy, and my heart swell out into the world beyond me, reaching all the way down to the earth below. I feel myself embracing our planet with my energy flow, with my open heart. I am without limits. All that exists up here is my consciousness, my open-ness, my far-reaching awareness. As I look affectionately down at our home below, my heart activated and full, I feel alive. I have let go. I have given myself over to my ever-expanding, all-encompassing energy, and I am truly free.

## Chapter 5
# Angels

Some people believe in angels, others don't. And even among the believers, opinions differ as to what an angel is. Regardless, reflecting on what an angel *represents* is possibly more telling than whether we do or don't believe in them. By visualizing an angel and inviting the ethereal energy that emerges into our life, into our hearts, we can imbibe their magic—and make them, at least somewhat, real.

So, what image comes to mind when *you* think of an angel?

I, personally, don't picture angels sitting quietly in meditation; I see them as busy beings of light, constantly on the move as they generate positivity and hope through selfless action. Yet, despite their on-the-move existence, they conduct themselves with absolute tranquility. In doing so, they represent how an active lifestyle can coexist with deep peace. They are the perfect illustration of stillness and love embedded in movement.

Let's imagine that angels really do exist—but instead of them being the celestial beings spoken about in spiritual texts, we'll have them be you and me during those times when our moods are bright, our energy levels are high, and love flows naturally from our eyes. We've all had those times, right? And these inspired moments in our life *surely* contain something of the divine within them—or, dare I say, angelic?

Let's be those angels, bringing light and inspiration to our world as we go about the bustle of our day.

## Becoming a Messenger of Light

There's nothing quite like seeing an image of the earth from space to give us a fresh perspective of our home—and a timely reminder of the poor job we are doing as trustees of this planet! Observing the earth's perfect floating sphere—with her beautiful array of blues and greens and browns—we'd be forgiven for thinking it's heaven we're looking at. Surely that immaculate pearl down there, drifting effortlessly through space, is the home of peace, love, and happiness for all?

Alas, our world isn't the paradise we dream of. So much so that we don't even have to look to war-torn countries to recognize how commonplace conflict is. Each one of us, no doubt, has our own everyday examples of tension and dissatisfaction, of the push and pull that accompany our daily existence.

So, how can we go about creating that very land of peace we so long for? Maybe the answer is simpler than we think. We are, after all, quick to forget how wide our very own circle of influence is. We forget how easily—how *instantly*—humans can instigate positive change. Just cast your mind back to the last time you met someone bursting with inspired energy. How did you feel in their presence? Good, I bet; positivity is contagious, after all!

The first step, therefore, in bringing about beneficial change and making our planet the beautiful place we wish for is to acknowledge that *we* are responsible for the change we wish to see. If we feel a lack of peace in our surrounds, then peace is what we need to emit.

How, then, do we step into this consciousness of being that author of positive change? One way is to reflect on our higher purpose here on earth. After all, we've surely not been given this privilege of life to merely tick off our daily to-do list—only to sleep, rise, and repeat it all tomorrow. *Surely* we have some higher spiritual purpose.

While considering our life's purpose—a big question, right?—we needn't feel overwhelmed by its apparent weight. There may, after all, not be one fundamental purpose to our life; we might find our reason for existence changes from day to day, from situation to situation. Right now, my role might be to offer love, while the following episode in my life may call for strength. As a result, a far more manageable question might be as follows: "In this moment, what quality is lacking in my immediate surrounds? What positivity could I offer to improve the atmosphere?"

By making a habit of reflecting on what is needed here and now, we may very well stumble first on our purpose (albeit a temporary one), and second upon the realization that we've been, very naturally, transformed into messengers of positive change.

It takes but one inwardly directed question, "What quality is lacking in my surrounds?" followed by a moment's quiet reflection in which we give our heart the space to emerge and offer that very quality. In doing so, we tap into inner spiritual guidance and are shown our path.

Another way we could frame this question is, "How can the universe utilize me right now?" or, "If I were an enlightened being, what qualities would surface in me to improve my surrounds?" It all comes back to opening up to our spiritual potential through looking within. And once we find our purpose, energy and momentum are quick to follow. Then we can start the healing process, both for ourselves and for the world.

Let's become those angels instrumental in transforming the world. Let's start with our immediate surrounds and bring well-being and beauty to this space, right now.

———

I bring myself into the present. Seated here in this chair, I become aware of my surrounds, of all the activity in my immediate environment and in my neighborhood. Being in constant interaction with nature and people, I have countless opportunities to shape my surrounds. I reflect for a moment on the typical influence I spread. How do I color the world? Do I bring a feeling of optimism? Of joy? Do I allow my inner light to shine when I am in contact with others? As a spiritual being on a spiritual path, this is what I wish for, after all. I wish to bring positivity through wholesome thinking, through benevolent feelings. I wish to emerge my qualities of peace and love and offer their beauty to the world. And so, in this moment, I consciously choose to be that instrument for positive change.

My first responsibility is to myself and this very space I find myself in. I start by looking within. And this simple act—observing my inner world—allows my light to reveal itself. And I see it, a warm glow inside. I feel its warmth. As I continue to study it, it begins to grow, begins to fill me. I feel its influence as it starts to filter through all parts of me. My entire body now glows with my very own warm, strong inner light. I instinctively know that there is a deep power in this light. It is a power I carry within, a power that I can use and share with the world.

For several moments, I simply appreciate this power at my disposal. I feel its strength, observing the influence it has on my inner world. I observe how easily it transforms me with its beauty, how it transforms my existence into something precious and impactful. Surely, then, if it can have such a positive effect on me, it can have an equally positive effect on my surrounds. So, I experiment. I offer my energy, my light, my power outward into my environment, and I watch as the area around me takes on a similar warm glow. I see the influence my light is having here, how it warms and improves this space. And when I am ready, I look to a place beyond my surrounds, to somewhere in my neighborhood, and I offer my light there. I nudge my light into that area and watch as its atmosphere is moved toward warmth and wholeness. And now I take my consciousness even farther outward, to a place beyond the earth—to beyond the physical and into the dimension of pure spirit. Up here, in this serene place of subtle light, I step into my role as a universal instrument. Here, in my calm, inspired state, I open myself up to the light that surrounds me, and I ask the universe,

"What energy can I offer the world? How can I, right now, be utilized in a divine way? How can I be a channel for beauty?"

And I give myself over to the universe, to higher light. I give myself over to powerful forces of the highest kind, and with total trust, I allow these forces to work through me. I let go to the universe, simply surrendering to the moment, surrendering to universal light. I let the highest light in and watch as it merges with my own light. And as light meets light, I become aware of a certain quality emerging within—perhaps peace, or love, or simply radiant beauty. I let go to this feeling entirely. I let it rise in my cells, in my heart, in my being. I let it flow, warming and filling me with its spirit. It spills out from me now, this essential light saturated with this quality. It streams out through my pores, beaming outward. As I release my energy, I bring radiant optimism into our world. I am a channel for goodness, for progress, for healing. I am a messenger of virtue, bringing positive change through light. I am an instrument of universal power, and this power moves through me, moves with me, and fills our world with sacred light.

## Revealing the Heart of an Angel

Walking meditations are perhaps the easiest introduction to angelic states; here, we learn how to bring spirituality into everyday action. Once we master bringing a spiritual mindset into a simple act like walking, we can progress to more complex acts like interacting with people while remaining aware of our inner being—of our powerful, light-filled mind.

Unfortunately, as we get swept up in living life, the first thing we forget *is* this inner light. That's where active reminders come into play; we need to talk to and encourage ourselves while going about our day. Set that hourly chime on your watch to remind yourself to whisper those words of personal guidance. Use your bathroom break as a reminder to step back inside and communicate with your highest self.

An inward conversation—with a dash of love—goes a long way toward bringing light.

⁓

As I set off on a walk, I purposefully slow my pace, allowing softness and smoothness to permeate my every movement. I enjoy this feeling of gentle motion, of my body operating with silky ease. I challenge myself to move even more smoothly, more gently, until it feels like I am not walking, but flowing forward. At the same time, I direct my focus inward, and I ask myself,

"How would an angel walk?"

I think of the gentleness and love filling each step of an angel, of the unhurried yet focused way they move about. And I bring those very angelic qualities into my gait. I walk softly, yet with focus. Immediately, I feel lighter on my feet. Each step is taken with love. Each footstep is unhurried. I feel my feet making quiet contact with the earth's surface. And yes, it's as though I really am just flowing forward. *Floating* forward. Again, I focus within, and I wonder about the heart of an angel. What feelings would emerge from that pure inner space of an angel? How unburdened would their experience of life be? I bring that angelic experience into my heart, those feelings of an angel into my being. I become that angel. I take a moment to reflect on what I must look like to the world right now. What kind of radiance do I, in my angelic state, emit? How bright my face must be! How serene my smile, how smooth my gait, how gentle my ambience.

Walking quietly forward, I allow my heart to exude its light outward. I allow my body to shine as an angel's would. I take every step in the consciousness that I am a moving, thinking, feeling angel. I am that very messenger of light. My steps are soft, my movements fluid. I am truly unburdened, unhurried, at peace. I feel a glow of clarity within my mind. My inner world is immaculately clean, and that purity, that clarity, reflects into my surrounds. Others can touch and feel it. This energy I emit is nothing more than a natural expression of a true heart, an effortless outpouring of light.

I now turn my gaze upward to the highest source of light. I look to the universal consciousness that is God. As an angel, my connection to God's light is natural and immediate. I simply shift my attention upward, and I am instantly connected to her light—to her warm, divine embrace. And as I keep moving forward, step after gentle step, I feel her light hovering over me, guiding me, keeping me focused on all that is positive and beautiful. I walk within her umbrella of light, constantly moving forward and upward with each step, constantly connected to her stream of love. Accompanied by God's light, I am kept on a path that always, always leads toward enlightenment.

I radiate as I move effortlessly forward. My inner light and God's light have merged. We are two powerful energies moving as one. I am with God, and I shine angelic purpose into my surrounds. I radiate with all the warmth and fullness of spiritual light.

## Awakening to the Fullness of Being

Our body, as an instrument operating within the laws of physics, has obvious limitations. We'd all love to fly like an eagle, or swim like a dolphin, or run like an antelope—but the physics of it all just doesn't add up!

So where *can* we achieve the seemingly impossible? In the field that lies beyond physics, of course—in the realm of spirit. The moment we move beyond our bodies and their limitations, we *can* fly. We can become—and experience—anything we wish for. By sitting quietly and placing our body in a dormant state, we can release our mind—our *spirit*—into a truly limitless world. And once there, unfettered, a simple word or phrase spoken lovingly to ourselves can transform the moment, taking us into the experience of our dreams. We can become precisely the person or the power we wish to be as we access our spiritual potential and release it into the fullness of being.

⌒

Sitting quietly, I slow down my breathing. With each inhalation, I breathe in calm energy, and with each exhalation, I let my body settle. I let it become heavier, let it simply fall into a restful state. Indeed, this state of rest and relaxation is none other than my body's default state. Just by letting it be, by stepping aside and observing the entirety of my body, I am returning it to its original condition of peace. And I do that; I observe my body, and with each successive in- and out-breath, I notice how it relaxes and loosens, how it becomes heavy, quiet, and settled. After a few more conscious breaths, I am satisfied that my body is still and calm. Silent. It has fallen into a dormant state.

I now imagine my body vanishing slowly, watching as it gradually becomes transparent, becomes lighter, as it fades, fades, fades away. It is barely visible now—and all of a sudden, my body is invisible. Gone. All that exists is my inner being. All I feel is pure spirit, pure consciousness. Here, deep inside, I am a fresh vessel, a clean slate upon which I can create beauty. My thoughts are my paintbrush. They are the energy through which I can manifest this beauty. My thoughts create my feelings and my experience, and thus my world. For that reason, I need to choose my thoughts carefully, to be conscious of what I am thinking.

In this moment, I choose to have a loving conversation with myself—a conversation that will lift me, inspire me, and color me with brilliance. I start by reminding myself who I am: light. I am conscious, living light. This light is warm. I know that because I can feel it here inside me. It spreads out, touching the entirety of my being. The light is healing and pure. I know that because I can feel its healing effect. I can feel how the light's pure vibration is guiding me toward complete health. This light inspires me, too, empowering me as it brightens my mind. I watch as it shines its glow through every part of me, spreading an atmosphere of wholeness, of peace, of vigor within. Inside, all is clear, and within this clarity, I realize my power. I can see and touch my highest potential. I do that, now; I reach out and touch the light. Immediately, my entire being ignites, and all is power and strength. In the fiery glow of it all, I am one with my highest, enlightened self. The light that explodes out around me is my energy, and this energy enhances, empowers, transforms.

As I observe this light radiating out from me, I realize that I am seated at the very center of this light. I am pure spirit, existing on a plane of light. And as spirit, I can become whomever I choose to be. I am simply one thought away from enlightenment, always. One thought away from perfect peace. Perfect love. Perfect bliss. I am a self-realized spiritual being. In this empowered state, a simple, focused thought is all the catalyst needed to take me into the highest, fullest experience. A simple thought in my spiritually awakened state carries with it a world of energy—energy that will guide me toward enlightenment. I think, and I become.

In order to tap into my potential, I choose the state I wish to be in right now. I choose the quality I want to fill myself with. If it's calm I wish for, I allow the energy of calm to fill my consciousness, to flow freely through me, to infuse itself in the glow that radiates within. And this glow, this calm, is as deep and wide and all-encompassing as the ocean, filling my entire being. It fills my consciousness, and my consciousness is without boundaries. I now let my mind and its calm light flow outward, into the farthest reaches of the world. The boundaries that previously existed between the world and me have vanished. My light flows freely outward, into open space, into nature, into others. I am here, and I am everywhere. I extend myself and my feelings as widely and as vibrantly as I wish.

My light has been set free into the world. My consciousness cascades outward, illuminating my surrounds. It serves as a beacon for others. They feel it—maybe even see it—and they draw their own inspiration from its positive vibration. I am an empowered being, bright and strong, and I offer my ever-expanding energy and light to the world.

## Brightening My Mind, Brightening the World

Every nook of our planet holds within it its own particular atmosphere—sometimes positive, sometimes neutral, and, yes, sometimes negative. This atmosphere influences our mood, even if only subconsciously. But at the same time, we're not innocent bystanders; we affect the atmosphere, too. We play our part in altering it—for the better, or for the worse.

So, what part am I playing in shaping my surrounds? What energy am I putting out there?

In the following exercise, we proactively place our awareness into a physical space we're about to enter and consciously influence its atmosphere with our warm vibration—*before* we even go in. We put our powerful energy out there, initiating change of the most positive kind.

⌒

Just before entering any physical space—be it my home, my office, a shop, or a bus—I first take myself there with my mind. By placing my consciousness there, it's as though I am already in that space. I start to get a feel for its interior. What atmosphere can I feel here? Is it positive or negative? Is it quiet or vibrant? And now, I ask myself, "How would I like to influence this atmosphere? What quality would light up its interior and make it a more inviting place for all?"

I become silent and look within for the answer. I find my inner power, my inner light, because it's this light that holds the key. Through my light, I can influence this space in a positive way. I trust my light to provide the right energy, the exact quality needed. To do so, I invoke the power of my inner light, looking into it and asking it to fill the void, to give what is lacking. And I listen to my light. Maybe I sense a deep silence emerging from within my light, or a feeling of peace, purity, or love. Whatever it is, I feel this quality rising within. I simply stand back and let my inner light surface—light that is saturated with silence, peace, or love. And I watch as this light fills me. I let it flood me with the full extent of its radiance.

Now, I allow the light to flow, just flow, from my inner world outward, into the place I am about to enter. I project this quality, this feeling into that space, sending my silence, peace, or love via my consciousness, via my vibration, via my light. I focus on this stream of energy emerging in me and cascading outward. I feel this river of light streaming out of me and entering the interior of that space and circling its way around. I can already sense the influence of my vibration there. I can feel how the atmosphere is being nudged toward positivity, toward beauty, toward light. I am a messenger for positive change, transmitting my clean energy, my bright influence, outward. And when I am ready, I physically step into this space.

As I enter, I take a moment to enjoy the atmosphere I have helped create. And this simple act of enjoying its mood attracts more light here—more positivity, more feeling. I bathe in the warmth of this atmosphere and trust that those around me, too, are comforted by its warmth.

# Chapter 6
## Healing

We all need a little healing from time to time, be it physically, emotionally, mentally, or spiritually. Healing is the process of becoming whole again—a return to our fully functioning, energetic, content self.

Let's harness meditation's power and initiate this shift back to wholeness. Let's ignite our original energy and see how close we can get to becoming complete.

## Firing Up My Healing Furnace

Meditation, although primarily considered a tool for mental and spiritual growth, is used in physical healing, too. Sceptics, of course, question the efficacy of an intellectual exercise like meditation on physical healing. Can the power of the mind really be applied to something so tangible as treating an injury or curing a disease? If we choose to believe the documented incidents of faith healing, it appears it can.

But let's suspend blind faith in others' experiences for a moment and go on our own journey of discovery. Let's delve into the laboratory of our mind, tap into its power, and find out for ourselves whether we can effect physical self-healing through the energy of the mind.

We will start with a minor pain, like a headache, a sore muscle, or a cough. Through purposeful thought, we'll open up our hearts, emerge the light, and embark on our experiment of energy healing.

———

I visualize my spiritual heart—that place deep below the surface, away from all the noise of the physical world. It's a private place that exists at the core of my being. I focus on this inner space and slowly fill it with light. I just let light emerge and grow within this space of my heart. Seeing how the light sparkles, feeling its cleanliness, I inherently sense its healing potential. And still the light pours in, filling my heart with its comforting, gentle radiance.

And I now let this light overflow, and into my body it spills. I let this nurturing spring of light stream out from my heart in a warm wave, like sacred water flowing out from the center of my being. I let it flow freely into my body, filling all its spaces, all its dark corners. I feel my heart's light moving down through my limbs, up through my chest, and into my head, finding every hidden nook and brightening my interior. I enjoy this soothing movement of energy within, its flow soft and calming.

I now turn my attention to any pain I may have—maybe a sore throat, knee, or shoulder, or a tight muscle—and allow this wave of warm energy, of warm light to flow there. As it moves into the area, I place my full trust in the light. I trust it to have the wisdom and power to heal. I trust it implicitly, because this light is imbued with the deep purity of spiritual substance. And spiritual substance, inherently, contains the most immaculate healing power.

So, with total trust, I direct my thoughts to the area that needs healing, and the light follows, flowing in. I continue to nudge the light in that direction with my consciousness, focusing the light's clean, nurturing energy in the area it's needed most. I feel the light filling this space with my very own molten healing energy. Immediately, I can sense this light and its gentle heat going to work, soothing the pain. I observe as the light nestles itself deeply into this area, massaging away the pain, the tightness, and rehabilitating it, making it new. I let more light in now, more therapeutic substance, and I feel the area becoming warmer and brighter until it becomes a healing furnace. I watch and feel as the heat works its way across the entire area, massaging its way deeper and deeper into my very cells. Surrendering to the light and the heat, I simply let healing happen. I watch the discomfort dissipating and the injury being healed. The pain is replaced by a comforting warmth, by glowing health.

I now release this flow of energy into my entire body, bringing holistic healing, brightness and light to every part of this physical instrument. The soothing flow of warmth nurtures me, bringing me back to vibrant, natural health.

## Summoning the Sweetest Sleep

Sleep is one of the great healers—while a *lack* of sleep is one of the great culprits in bringing dis-ease. We all know the feeling of getting into bed only to be kept awake by racing thoughts—that, when all we're wishing for is to slip into restful slumber! The following short visualization exercise clears our mind of these pesky distractions, offering us a pathway into deep, peaceful sleep.

As I lie in bed, I let my focus drift inward to the inner workings of my body. I take a few moments to inspect my inner physical world. While doing so, I imagine a light emerging at the center of my being. I let this light intensify and become bigger and brighter. As it grows in me, I release it through my eyes, two beams of light streaming outward.

Again, I direct my vision inward, and as I continue surveying the inside of my body, glancing from side to side, my vision casts these beams of gentle light on everything in its path. I shower every corner of my interior with this light, clearing the dust and bringing clarity. My vision leaves every space empty, quiet, and clean. As I continue to look left and right, sweeping my inner world with light, I feel my body being ushered toward a state of deep relaxation. My body is feeling comfortable and heavy, just about ready to be swallowed by sleep's warm embrace. I let my body be—just let it go, let it rest.

I now direct the light of my vision into the room of my mind. Here, too, as I glance around, swishing my beams of light to and fro, I clear my head of all disturbances. I feel it becoming empty and silent. My mind is at rest, in a state of warm comfort. My mind—and my body—are now comfortable and quiet. Clean and relaxed. Soft and still. I am settled, and my inner world glows with golden, soothing light. In this contented state, I am ready to sink into deep slumber. I let go, following that gentle call toward peaceful, contented sleep. I feel myself drifting forward into sleep's warm, welcoming embrace.

## Being Moved by the Magic of Music

Music, with all the images and associations it conjures up in us, can move us physically, emotionally, and even spiritually. It can bring serenity or sadness to the moment, uplift and excite us, or fill our hearts with nostalgic longing. It has the power to change the direction of our thoughts and mood in an instant.

In the following exercise, we let music do just that: move us. We dive into its flow and harness its power. Depending on the experience we're after, we can choose our music accordingly. Feel like an exciting, vibrant experience? Go for something upbeat. Want some calm? Find something a little more subdued and peaceful.

Let's turn it up and tune in.

———

I sit still and focus on the music. I consciously flick my internal switch to *receptive*, enabling my body, my being, my consciousness to become a vessel capable of absorbing all. In this open, ready state, I start to feel the music as it fills my surrounding space. I hear it, yes, but I go deeper into it, picking up on the intricacies of its sounds floating within touching distance of me, on the notes that bounce about in their own beautiful dance. I observe the variety of sounds, making up the complex assembly that is this song.

All these individual notes, these beautiful sonic vibrations, are like a whirlwind swirling around me. I follow their flow as they circle around the outskirts of my head, and I surrender to them. I give myself over to the music's vibration, to its energy, and in doing so, I let it flow into me. I feel my body absorbing the multitude of different sounds—their textures, their colors, their pulse. I feel the music seeping into my limbs, my torso, my head. The sounds are inside me now, swimming through me, all the notes in flight, alive, in motion. They massage my muscles as they sweep into every corner of my body. The beat, the rhythm, the sounds all nurture, all cleanse and heal.

The music is a vibration inside me, a dynamic energy moving through me like a river on its own magical path. It's a river that brings cleanliness and vitality to my inner world. I simply follow its sounds as they move on their independent journey inside me. I observe them, feel them, let them fill my body with their sparkle and might. As the music touches the depths of my being, I feel it working its magic on me and into me with its harmony and flow.

## Emerging the Energy of the Cells

Through the power of our imagination, we can travel not only outward to far-off places, but inward, too, exploring the miracle of our body. We can go as deep as ever—directly into our cells, if we wish—to get a feel for that ever-present spring of energy keeping our body balanced and alive.

Let's become those inward voyagers and take a peek at the inner workings of this incredible physical instrument we inhabit.

———

I take a deep breath and dive into my body, entering my muscles, my organs, my bloodstream. I feel myself floating around within, going to all parts of my body as I explore the inner workings of my physical being. How vast it is down here! And now I go deeper still, into my cells.

Within these building blocks of my body, I sense the stirring of a life force, the very essence of my physical vitality. I enter an individual cell now and observe firsthand this force that is so instrumental in keeping my body ticking over. I observe the magic of this tiny cellular pocket of life, bursting with substance and vigor. This cell holds a lively charge, radiating with its own energy, its own light. It produces its own vibration, its own hearty Om.

I rest here within this individual cell and become acutely aware of this healthy throb of energy emanating from its center. I feel it emerging and flowing outward from the cell, sending ripples into my body.

I now take a step back, exiting this cell to appreciate the totality of all my cells as they work in harmony to fuel and activate my body. Each one pulses with its own sacred Om. Each one emits its own special energy, an energy that overflows into its surrounds. As all my cells' energy rolls out into my body, I consciously reabsorb it back into my cells, soaking up the vibrant power being released by each cell. I bathe in this healing vibration that pulses out from me, then reenters me, and I let go into the fullness of the experience. I give over to the robust Om emerging inside my cells, flowing out, then back in.

I turn my attention to a part of my body needing healing, and just by being conscious of that area, already this cellular energy, this river of essential Om flows there. I immediately feel a rich warmth merging in that area as my inner flow of energy streams into it, congregating and saturating it with power. I let this healing energy, this sacred Om, ease and nourish this part of my body. I sit back and simply observe the radiant energy doing what it does best: healing through vibration, through warmth, through light. This restorative energy is within me, filling and nourishing me with its flow. I let go to its healthy pulse and allow the purest, most natural healing to happen. I surrender, willingly, to my inner, vibrant, nurturing Om.

## Self-Healing through Love

We all need, at one point or another, some form of physical therapy, be it for an ankle, a hip, a headache, or even a disease. Whatever it is, we can assist the healing process through directing the right energy—*focused* energy—toward the pain center. And what is the right energy? Love, of course, offered via a gentle conversation with the very part of our body crying out for our attention.

I go within and direct my focus toward a part of my body needing attention. Wherever I have pain or discomfort, that's where I go. I move my awareness into this area and rest there for a moment, just sitting next to the pain. Sitting with the pain.

"I see you," I say, with absolute sincerity, to the part of my body in pain. "I truly see you," I say with love. "I acknowledge you and your pain. You are part of me, and so I know you are there. I know you are hurting. But I am here, too. I am next to you. I am with you. We'll get through this together. Everything will be okay; I promise."

I focus on the area of discomfort and go deeper into it. I see the individual cells making up this area and direct my energy, my thoughts, toward these cells.

"I am right here with you in your pain. I love you, and I am beside you. I can heal you. I can give you the warmth, the energy you need to heal. I can give you love. Here—feel this warmth I am sending you right now. Feel my energy. Feel my love."

And I send every cell in the area my warmth, my energy, my love. I feel a gentle comfort surfacing there, a vibration that is filled with healing energy. Slowly but surely, I feel healing happening as my energy continues to flood the area with warmth. I watch as this part of my body shifts toward wholeness, as it returns to a state of newness.

"I am with you," I repeat, continuing to send my thoughts, my vibration, my power to this area. I continue to heal myself from within, with love.

## Surrendering to the Sound of Om

We are surrounded by a host of different sounds throughout the day, some pleasant, others less so. While few of us would begrudge the gentle gurgle of a stream or the chirping of birds, some sounds, like the banging and crashing of a nearby construction site, can be hard on the ears. Nonetheless, even unpleasant sounds can be transformed into something positive if we consider them to be nothing more than a series of vibrations—or deep, resonating Oms. If you've ever heard the buzz of cicadas in summer, you could liken these Oms to that—an endless outpouring of little vibrations.

By making a small attitude shift, we can open ourselves up to auditory vibrations and enjoy a healing, uplifting massage anytime of the day!

I close my eyes and become aware of the sounds around me. I realize there is an auditory amphitheater out there, each sound different, each one coming from another direction. I focus on one sound—maybe the buzz of insects, the drone of traffic or machinery, the hum of my computer, the babble of voices, the whooshing of wind, or the thrumming of rain. The more I focus on this one sound, the more I realize it's nothing more than a series of energy pulses, of vibrations, of tiny audio pockets coming my way. These individual vibrations, these particles of sound, are like little Oms—wavelets splashing up against me. I feel their sounds and their vibrations entering me through my skin, seeping inward.

I invite this endless, tactile stream of sound vibrations in, watching as they pass through me, into the deepest reaches of my body. I follow these pulses' inward flow, enjoying their massaging power as they work themselves through the corridors of my inner world. I feel them entering my muscles, flowing down my legs and into my toes, my arms, my fingers, and up through my chest. I open myself up to this series of deep, satisfying Oms moving into me, moving through me, massaging me, nourishing me. I let the sound and the vibration of Om fill me. I let it calm me, let it knead my muscles and heal me. I let it energize me. The vibration of Om is within me, and it flows freely through me. My entire being is filled with its sound, and I enjoy its stream of uplifting energy. I give myself over to the deep, healing massage of Om.

## Reawakening My River of Life

Being conscious of what's happening inside our body is a quick, effective way to escape the mental chatter that sometimes clutters our head. This exercise in self-awareness brings us into the present while relaxing us, too.

Let's dive inward and listen to that peaceful yet dynamic world that exists beneath our skin, venturing off on a pilgrimage to our very own retreat center within.

———

I wish to know more about the workings of my inner world. To do so, I need to go there. I need to be inside and experience its corridors, its vistas, firsthand. To do so, I dive beneath my skin, into that deep ocean within. And immediately, I find myself seated, almost magically, here at the center of my body. I take several moments to accustom myself to my surrounds, listening for any sounds that exist within this unseen world, for any noises or vibrations being emitted. I may feel or even hear my own heartbeat, or the gentle purr of my energy flow as it goes about its business across the length and breadth of my body. Or maybe all I sense is a deep, calming silence.

By just being here and listening to my internal environment, I am forging an intimate relationship with my body. I am getting in touch with the inner workings of this wonderful instrument, getting to understand it on a deeper level. A sense of stillness envelops me down here; I am so entirely removed from the outside world and its flurry of activity. That noise and movement—it's all so far away. Right now, I am here in my own cocoon of stillness and comfort within. I am seated in my very own sanctum, separated from all outside influence. It's just my physical body and me. The conscious me. The me who right now is aware of this body as a moving, feeling, tactile instrument existing around me. And here at the center of my body, all is at peace; all is quiet.

While observing my body and its inner world, I become aware of the internal processes keeping my body alive—those synchronized, smooth actions and reactions happening around me. As I listen to these processes, I realize there's a soothing hum to all this living energy down here. This is the hum of life: the resonance of my robust inner flow of energy moving through my body. How comforting it is to experience my very own physical life force in this way. How therapeutic it is to feel this vibration as it rolls its way through me.

This vibration is my very own sacred inner hum, moving like a breathing, vibrant river through all parts of my body. I observe its flow down my legs, into my arms, up my back, into my head. This deep resonance fills and nourishes me. I trust in its wisdom to heal. This energy knows what my body needs, after all. Its role is to harmonize, to energize, to bring life. This vibration dissolves blockages, opens passageways, and flows into the spaces that emerge, bringing oxygen, bringing vitality. I feel my body radiating from within with this shifting, healing, uplifting hum. And as this deep resonance rises to the surface, my skin tingles with its gentle rumble.

I sit quietly, an observer inside my body, taking these moments to witness and appreciate my inner health-giving, primary vibration. I let it flow, and the flow is inherently good, innately wise. I let go to it, just rolling with its warm vibrancy. I release myself into the fullness of my river of life within, letting it purge, letting it heal, letting it flow.

## Restored by the Flow Within

One of the greatest gifts we have been given as tiny sparks of spiritual life is no doubt the human body. We are seated in a thinking, talking, moving instrument with five electrically sharp senses at our disposal. Just reflecting on the staggering complexity of this physical instrument can be a useful exercise in gratitude as we marvel at its composition of skeletal, muscular, and nervous systems—never mind all that is happening on a cellular level! These physical elements, all working together in one seamless process with the sole objective of giving life, are nothing short of a miracle.

Let's venture inward and get a firsthand glimpse of our body and its river of life that flows so naturally, so constantly, within.

———

Living in a world as dynamic as ours, I am constantly brought back to the awareness of all that is happening in my surrounds—all the sounds, the movements, the hustle and bustle as life plays itself out around me. But I'm not always so aware of what is happening inside this body I inhabit. Yet it's a body I can retreat into at any time. Deep within, there is that safe space always waiting to welcome me. And I choose to do so now. I slip neatly and quietly within, going beneath my skin to observe the inner workings of my body.

The first thing I notice is how silent it is down here. It's as though I've dived into a lake's silent, deep waters. I take a moment to listen to the hush that exists here below the surface. I sense a profound peace; everything around me is so still, so rested. I spend several moments just appreciating this quiet atmosphere down here, as well as appreciating the effect this silence has on me. Just resting here, being still and present, I am being filled, being satisfied. I now continue my inner exploration, and down into my legs I go. I feel the flow of energy that exists there, this life force moving through my legs, and I enjoy its vibrancy, its fluidity. I take a moment to appreciate the comfort this energy offers as it circulates down through my legs, into my toes, then back up and into my thighs, my hips, before repeating its cyclical flow. I follow this circular stream of energy, observing the healing it brings to the lower parts of my body as it meanders smoothly through them. I focus on an area of my legs that may feel stiff or sore—maybe my ankles, or knees, or hips—and watch as energy spills through this area, its warmth massaging these parts. I feel an immediate relief there, a gentle release of tension, an opening up of the entire area. I return my attention to my legs as a whole and take a moment to appreciate the sensation of well-being that has settled in them.

I now observe this energy as it moves upward, following it as it shifts the direction of its flow toward my stomach. And again, I feel the life force it carries. I feel its healing power as it circulates within my stomach. I feel how any stomach or digestive issues are soothed and simply washed away within its energizing flow.

Now, in my own time, I follow its journey to all the other dark, silent corners of my body: my chest, my shoulders, my arms, my neck, my head. As I move within this warm stream, its contents bursting with health-giving substance, I am given a firsthand view of the areas it enters and the healing it carries out. I watch the various parts of my body being returned to health in the most natural way possible. I feel it massaging my entire body. This energy leaves a warmth in its wake, a gentle throb that invigorates and purifies. Observing the healing happening in me, I feel a deep sense of gratitude for this inner flow of energy, filling me and helping restore this beautiful instrument of my body to glowing health.

## Returning to My Beautiful Self

Many of us spend a large portion of our lives living outside ourselves. We project ourselves via our thoughts into the past or the future or into the world around us. We worry about what happened yesterday or what might happen tomorrow or what others may be thinking about us right now. In the process of all this noise, we fall into a kind of unconscious state, removed from the *I* of it all.

The following exercise brings us back into the present and back to ourselves. We return to our essence via one simple question: "How am I feeling right now?" Interestingly, the response that surfaces seems always to be a positive one; somehow, this inwardly directed question invokes a virtue, manifesting itself as a good feeling within. A hint of peace may emerge, or contentment, stillness, or love.

By practicing this basic yet empowering self-awareness exercise, not only do we prompt a positive inner response, but we are pulled back to the present and to our hearts. It's here that we reunite with the essential *I* at center of our being.

⌒

I acknowledge that sometimes I neglect my relationship with myself. Sometimes I even forget who the real me is. And now it's time to reconnect with that beautiful life form that is me. What I need is a vivid reminder of my incredible potential via an experience of myself as that being of spirit, of essence, of light. I start by directing my focus to the space that exists in my heart. I ask myself,

"How am I feeling right now?"

I take a moment to listen to my inner environment, opening myself up to any tingling sensation I may feel within. Whatever emerges, I welcome it. I acknowledge and feel it. And now, I probe a little deeper:

"What is the atmosphere inside me like?"

I listen for that inner vibration in whatever form it may surface.

"What quality is contained within this vibration, within this energy that I am emitting right now?"

It may be peace that I feel, or love, stillness, contentment, or power. Whatever feeling emerges, the more I listen to it, the more it grows. And I let it grow. I let it swell within me. I let it expand and fill me. I let it become me. I am this radiant quality. I am composed entirely of this. As this extraordinary feeling continues to spread through me, I surrender to it. I let it take over and fill me. I let it flow through me like a river that soothes, that warms, that gives. I become one with this feeling that exists at the center of my being, that exists throughout me as it streams out across the length and breadth that is me. Keeping my gaze turned inward, I observe a world that is filled with radiance and virtue. I am seeing my very own existence, and all is beautiful within.

## Seated in the Path of the Sun

On a cold winter day, is there anything more pleasurable than settling down in a sunny spot and absorbing all that golden, solar goodness? Just thinking about it is enough to brighten our mood!

In the same vein, we can warm our *inner* world by placing ourselves into the path of spiritual light. By turning our awareness to God's energy and absorbing her light, we can fill ourselves with healing, spiritual sunlight.

Let's find ourselves a comfy spot directly in the path of that highest, transformative light.

———

I cast my attention skyward to the sun. I think of its potent energy, of the warmth it gives our planet. I think of its beams of radiant light showering goodness down onto us. I think of how it unconditionally sustains all forms of life on earth. And now, I think of God's light. I think of the similarities between her spiritual light and the sun's. Both are nourishing, warm, and essential. Both provide life, and both give, constantly.

I visualize God as that beautiful, glowing sun. I watch as energy radiates out from her center and streams down toward the earth. And I put myself in the path of her energy, her light. I catch the fullness of its flow as it lands squarely on me. In an instant, I know I am being touched by a substance from some enchanted realm. This energy, unlike anything I've experienced here in the physical world, is clearly from another dimension, from a world of pure spirit, pure light. I feel a distinct tingling on the crown of my head where God's rays of sunshine are landing so abundantly. I allow the sensation to filter in through my scalp and flow into me like molten gold. Her shimmer curls deep into my body, a shimmer that feels so nourishing and good. I open myself up to this highest light, letting more of it in, letting it stream deep into my body, down through my limbs until it finds my toes.

My body is like a bucket, catching this pure light as it spills down from above. I simply let it in, let it happen, let this miracle of energy flow into me from above. The light has settled in my feet now, warming me from the bottom reaches of my body. Having filled my feet, God's radiance starts to rise into my legs, now settling in the lower half of my body. I feel the change that has taken place from my waist down, a warm, healing comfort filling the lower half of my body. As the light continues its inward flow, trickling up each successive part of my body, I watch as the healing continues. Light settles in my stomach—now my chest, my back, my arms, my hands and fingers, my neck. I observe its effect as it permeates each area with its clean glow. Moving gradually upward, it leaves a gorgeous tingling in its wake. And now it flows into my face, golden light filling my cheeks, my eyes, my forehead. My scalp bristles with its nurturing energy.

I look down and see that my entire body is radiating with light now, flickering with health. I take as long as I wish to just sit back and enjoy this spectacle, this feeling, this glow. This is God's divine energy, entering our world from the hallowed realm of spirit and streaming onto me, into me, circulating through me as it continues its journey of deep healing. I let the totality of this miracle sink in: right now, I am being filled with the highest, most transformative light in existence. I feel the exquisite gravity of that fact as the light concentrates and pools up in any problem area I may have. I simply let the warmth fill that area, let it soothe and heal. Soothe, and heal. Energize, and restore. My body is glowing with vitality, and this vitality is so rich, so real, so wholesome.

Finally, when I am ready, I let this light overflow. I let it splash outward into my environment, onto everything around me. I become aware of how good it feels to give, to be a donor of light. I have received God's light, taken it in, and let it heal me. And now I offer it to my surrounds. As light streams out from me, I observe this cycle of energy: light flowing down into me, through me, and out of me, into my environment. I am filled with the splendor of divine light. I feel how it invigorates me, lifts me, makes me whole. And in releasing it, I let it continue its purposeful path outward, bringing abundance and renewal to my surrounds.

## Opening My Palms to the Light

In natural healing circles, the hands—particularly the palms—play an important role, serving as that energy medium between healer and patient. But it's not only "healers" who are blessed with healing potential; we are *all* healers, whether we actively use our gift or not. Healing energy flows through every one of us; we simply need to put it to use, to actively summon it in our pursuit of regeneration and growth. And when we do choose to access this inner power, not only do we realize our vast potential in spreading positive influence, but we become more in tune with and open to our inner worlds, too. The very act of accessing our healing energy leads us to our core, revealing the depths of our subtle, spiritual side.

In order to get a feel for the efficacy and potency of our healing energy, all we need to do is open our hands and pay attention to our palms; in most cases, that energy will make itself known to us within seconds, often as a comforting, warm glow in the center of each palm.

Try it for yourself: open those palms, feel the glow, and get a sense of the powerful energy lying in wait, ready to shift yourself and the world toward wholeness and health.

———

Sitting down, I open both hands, turning my palms upward. I become aware of a gentle buzz above each palm, almost as though a soft, comforting weight has settled on each hand. Focusing on my palms, I let this energy, this weight, become fuller, heavier, warmer. I take several moments to simply appreciate this vibration emerging from the center of each palm. Something has awakened there, and I feel it.

I now imagine a great light above me—or, if I am outdoors, I connect to the sun—and I catch this light on my palms. Pure energy streams down onto me, pure light, and I absorb it through my open hands. I welcome this golden light onto and into my palms, and I feel as it funnels in, moving gorgeously up my arms and into my entire body. It warms me, this light, and it nourishes and strengthens my core.

Again, I focus on the energy bubbling up on my palms, decidedly stronger and fuller now. And I realize it's time to give. To do so, I raise my hands very slowly, turning my palms outward. I take this moment to offer light to the world through my hands, letting pure energy wash out through my palms and into my surrounds. These are healing hands, and I use them to distribute light. As I continue to absorb light from above and send it outward through my palms, I take a moment to appreciate the importance of my hands and their role in giving, in healing. With arms aloft, still receiving light from above, I shower clean energy onto the world. In it comes, out it goes. I am a spiritual conduit, caught up in this beautiful flow of living, healing light.

## Nudging My Body
## toward Wholeness and Health

Our bodies, when given the chance, have an astonishing capacity for self-healing. Unfortunately, poor habits (read *unhealthy diets and sedentary lifestyles*) limit this healing potential.

Our mind, too, can play a role in shifting us toward physical health. By bringing ourselves into a quiet, calm state, then focusing powerful beams of mental energy on any aches and pains we may have, we can assist the healing process.

Let's access this mental energy and put it to good use as we coax our bodies back toward newness and health.

⁓

I silence myself via a few slow, gentle breaths. In, and out. Gently in, slowly out. With the next inhalation, I follow my breath as it flows inward, letting it lead me into the depths of my body. And here within, I take a moment to listen to my body. Where is healing needed? Where can I feel tension? What part is out of balance? My stomach, maybe? Or my eyes? Maybe all that's needed to restore physical health is relaxing that very area, enabling any inner blockages— created by the tension I'm holding there—to loosen up, to dissolve. Blockages prevent the flow of healing energy, after all, and I need my healing energy to flow.

Having identified where renewal is needed, I focus solely on that area. And just the act of taking my attention there results in an instant pooling of energy as warmth flows in, so primed and eager is my body to start the healing process. This influx of energy may be in the form of crisp, sparkling light; or a warm red glow; or a cool blue flame. It may simply be a comforting buzz. Whatever mode my healing energy takes, I give it full license to surface in all its potency and abundance. I let it flow, unencumbered, into the area needing to be restored. As the energy wells up there, as warmth floods in, I feel this area of my body taking nourishment from the inward flow. I feel the muscles around the area hungrily absorbing the clean energy, and before I know it, the entire area has responded with a wholesome glow. Warmth continues to flow in, and as more energy is absorbed, the cells in the area start to respond. I feel them begin to vibrate with a healthy rumble, and I realize that what I am hearing is my very own cells' vibrant life force reawakening. And within that rumble lies even greater healing potential.

For a moment, I focus on that pulse emerging from my cells, on its healing power, on the effect this power is having on the surrounding area. I feel my blood circulation in that area opening up, too, as blood flows naturally and freely in and around it, between the pulsating cells, unlocking any blockages and opening up my natural healing pathways. I observe in wonder as this area is being brought back toward health.

I now let this inner healing glow spread to all regions of my body. I step back and allow its wholesome flow to move freely up and down my legs, through my torso and arms, and into my head. A sensation of well-being mushrooms through my entire being, now shining with blissful, radiant health. I am full, and my body glows with life.

## Being Comfortable in My Skin

Many of us spend much of our lives living outside ourselves, concerned more with what's happening around us than inside us. While remaining conscious of the outside world is by no means a bad thing, we'd be better off investing more of our precious time appreciating and polishing our treasured worlds within.

For this internal awareness and growth to happen, we need a regular, conscious practice of turning our focus inward and observing what is happening within. As we become accustomed to getting glimpses of the silent depths of our being, we build a natural stock of internal peace and stability, and we can truly become the embodiment of the phrase "comfortable in my skin."

⸻

I imagine my body to be like a protective casing into which I can slip whenever I wish. Right now, I choose to do that. In I go, withdrawing into this outer shell of my body, into its safe, womblike interior. I settle myself very naturally, deep within my core, enjoying the feeling of warmth and comfort. I am secure and content here, in my quiet inner space beneath the surface. Being within and conscious of my inner world, I have instant access to all parts of my body. I can travel around inside and iron out any creases, soothe any areas of tension, release any pockets of blocked energy. Just by taking my consciousness and its dynamic, vibrant energy to different parts of my body and pausing for a moment in a specific area, I can bring immediate healing and instant peace.

To start this process, I scan my body right now, and I identify any hot spots needing attention. I look for areas of tension or pain. And I move to one such area, taking my awareness, my glow of life there. And once I arrive, I rest there. Simply by seating myself in this space, I notice an immediate lifting of tension and an easing of pain. Just being here, comfortably settled in this specific part of my body with full consciousness, allows transformation to happen. And I watch that healing unfold, relishing this very natural shift toward wholeness. When I am satisfied that this part of my body is sturdy and sound, I move to another area requiring healing, another area calling for my gentle yet powerful spiritual focus. I go there with my mind and energy and, again, simply rest there and let restoration happen.

One by one, I visit all the stressed parts of my body, consciously being there, being present, attending to each area needing my attention. Through this practice, I'm able to connect to and spend meaningful time with different parts of my body. I bring warmth and healing through my presence. I bring peace.

Once I have moved through all the areas of my body needing attention, I take a moment to notice the totality of it all, of my entire body in this whole state. I notice that a feeling of relaxation has settled throughout me. A warm, even flow of energy runs through me, circulating smoothly and easily across the planes of my inner world. My body is deeply settled, comfortably warm, tension-free. The only moving part of my being is this inner flow, this river of soothing, healing energy. I take a deep breath in, then release it in a slow, satisfied exhalation. Sitting still, enjoying this moment, I appreciate the harmony I feel within.

## Inviting the Light In

When we think of a cave, we think of a space devoid of light. Yet all it takes is a single hairline crack connecting the bright outside world to its dark interior to illuminate it completely.

In the same way, the recesses of our body and mind are like a dark cave yearning for illumination. A spark of light may be just what's required to recharge and reinspire those vast inner spaces of both body and mind.

In the following exercise, we ignite that spark within, splashing our inner worlds with inspiring light.

———

I sit quietly, eyes closed, and imagine the inside of my body to be like a cave, cool and dark. I take some time to appreciate the soothing stillness within, the gentle peace filling this dark space. But maybe it's time to change the mood, to transform my inner environment into something more active, to inject some vigor. Yes, now's the time to brighten up my inner space. And so, with the wish to bring in light—and with the light, renewal—I imagine my closed eyes to be like the cracks in the walls of the cave. And ever so slowly, I begin to open my eyes.

As the first slivers of light filter inward, I observe their beams curling down into my torso. I watch as these rays of light reach my feet and toes, feel them seeping down into my hands and fingers. I notice a wondrous transformation happening. I see, firsthand, the effect the incoming light has as it touches the inner recesses of my body with its crisp, vibrant energy. I feel the beauty and fullness of this light as it flows in, filling my entire being with its sparkle. I give myself time—as much as I need—to fully appreciate the revitalization that is taking place within, to enjoy this shift from darkness toward light.

And now, having offered my body this deep, rich cleanse, I turn my attention toward my mind. I direct these same beams of light into the recesses of my thinking world, into the room of my mind. I let light flow straight into the center of my consciousness, and the effect is one of immediate clarity. The once-dark space of my mind now shimmers with clean light, and my mood is instantly lifted. I allow more light in, observing and appreciating the effect this flood of radiance has on my mood. The light, so pure and powerful, clears my mind and lifts me. I feel new, refreshed, inspired.

Energized, I turn my attention back to my body, marveling at its clean state. I look into my mind and feel its bright interior. The light has cleansed me, lifted me, given me clarity. I carry a world of light within and brim with its fullness and strength.

## Healing through Sound

Nature has an array of different sounds, some of which have an especially soothing quality to them; just think of the swish of the ocean, the pitter-patter of rain, or the rustling of leaves in a light breeze. How good these sounds make us feel!

Let's incorporate some similarly gentle sounds into our meditation and have them whisk us off to a beautiful place.

I sit quietly, allowing my body to relax. Moments later, having brought myself into a restful state, I open my ears to the sound of my own breath moving softly in, softly out, smoothly in, smoothly out. I now go within, sliding with ease into my body and tuning in to my heartbeat. Even if I can't physically hear it, I imagine the sound it makes in my chest. I hear its deep, rhythmic beat, and I take a moment to appreciate its consistency, its strength.

As I move closer to this sound, to its stable beat, it becomes louder and fuller. Now, taking one final step inward, I find myself right at the center of my heart, its reverberation resounding all around me. I feel the force in its beat—that deep pulse being pushed out with metronomic consistency. I feel its resonance booming across my entire body. It feels so good, this inner beat and its full, bodily vibration. I sense the power of my heart and feel somehow protected here inside it.

Now, from this space within, I open myself up to a different sound coming from some other region of my inner world. It is the crisp sound of a wind chime. *Cling!* Its echo swirls around inside me for several seconds. *Cliiing!* It comes again, and I pick up on the series of vibrations making up this very cling. I follow these vibrations as they move through my body. And another fresh chime—*cling!* Each one reverberates through the full length of my body, massaging me with its pristine, clear sound. *Cling!* This time, I trace the sound to its source inside my body. I locate its origin. Again, it comes—*cling!*—emerging from this specific place within before pealing outward delightfully across my body. It leaves in its wake a clean resonance—sharp at first, then slowly fading into silence. Again it rings out, and I feel the clarity of these bright notes and their vibration as they move through me. I listen more carefully to the next chime, moving closer to get a deeper feel for what it's composed of. *Cling!* I notice it's made up of thousands of tiny tremors, each one carrying its own vibration that streams through me. I observe the cleanliness left in their path, these pockets of sound penetrating the different parts of my body, touching and soothing me. Their vibrations are like droplets of pure love, caressing me.

Chime after chime, the sounds peal out from within, their pulses flowing meticulously through my entire body. A feeling of wholesomeness is left in their wake, as well as a subsequent vigor. The chimes and their vibrations lift my body, leaving me tingling with health. They are purifying me from within, and I glow from the fullness and beauty of each successive chime. I shine with the delicate ringing that moves in me and through me, cleaning and lifting every aspect of my being with its crisp sound.

# Chapter 7
## Grounding

"Just stay grounded, and you'll be okay!" Ever heard that advice only to find yourself wondering exactly what it means to be in a "grounded" state?

Staying grounded is about remaining true to your original self—and living that truth. It's about being the authentic you and not getting caught up in a false ego. It's also about staying connected to the practical reality of living in the real world. And what better return to reality is there than spending time in nature, experiencing the soil at our feet and the earth as it exists around us.

By connecting to nature, we take ourselves back to what is true, original, and, yes, natural. We ground ourselves like a tree as we connect with this planet's energy and feel it bringing us warmly back down to earth.

Let's be that grounded tree—deeply rooted, unshakably strong, and constantly true.

## Exploring the Energy of the Earth

Considering the earth is where we live out the entirety of our physical reality, it's easy to take her for granted. Yet this is the planet that provides near-perfect conditions for millions of species to exist and flourish. Now isn't that amazing!

By being attentive to the wonder of having this great planet located right beneath our feet, we're able to tap into her veritable spring of life. We can channel her energy into us and ground ourselves in the most powerful way.

———

Standing or sitting (preferably barefoot), I place both feet firmly on the ground. I become aware of the contact point between the soles of my feet and the earth's surface, and I instantly feel a gentle, tingling sensation where my feet meet the earth. Simply by touching the earth in this way, I am able to detect the earth's deep energy and forge a connection to that clean, sustaining force she so readily emits. And I feel that force, right now, through the soles of my feet.

As I go deeper into this tickling sensation beneath my feet, I notice the energizing effect it is having on me. It's like there's a play of electricity dancing on the soles of my feet, sending an invigorating flow of life up my legs. I take my focus to the earth now, to that great mass of elements beneath my feet, and I go below her surface to her depths. Because down there, I know, lies the source of this very energy streaming up my legs. And I move toward the earth's core, where this energy is at its strongest. I move toward the very origin of the earth's incredible energy, and the deeper I go, the more I become aware of the great power that exists at the center of our planet. I feel her rumbling vibrancy, a vibrancy that contains the life-giving potential for so many species to flourish on her surface. I take a moment to rest there, deep within the earth's belly, and surround myself with her colossal energy.

Sitting here at her center, experiencing her power first-hand, I get a true feel of her immensity, an appreciation for the magnitude of it all. Now, very gradually, I take myself back to the earth's surface and back to that tingling on the soles of my feet. Knowing the origin of this delicate sensation—that resounding might within the earth's core—I draw from that power. The tingling grows stronger and more intense, and once again I feel it entering me through my feet and moving up my legs.

As it flows upward, all the way into my torso now, I observe the effect this earth energy is having on my entire body. I watch in wonder as it washes in, caressing me, cleaning me, empowering me. I fill myself with its force, not reading anything into it, instead just enjoying the inner flow, the warmth, the vigor as it gushes delightfully in. I am being washed clean by its might. I consciously open myself up further, allowing this earth energy to penetrate deeper, to seep into the cells of my body. And on this cellular level, I feel renewal happening, transformation unfolding. Each individual cell of my body is being charged with clean, potent energy. I feel alive, my body energized and brimming with strength. I hold on to the fullness of the vibration glowing within, onto this life-sustaining energy that continues its inward flow.

Right now, here on the surface of the earth, I am divinely connected to our beautiful planet, absorbing her energy and filling myself with her power. I intimately understand the constancy and vibrancy of the earth's life-giving force, and I feel truly grateful for this planet we call home.

## Experiencing the Thrill of Flight

Who among us hasn't dreamed we are flying, only to wake up wishing it were true! As humans, we seem to have an inherent desire to glide above the earth, freeing ourselves into the weightless beauty of flight.

If we put our imaginations to good use, the feeling of flying can become more than a dream. We can step into the world of that irrepressible eagle, soaring effortlessly through the air. All that's required is that we close our eyes, open our wings, and release our minds into the vastness of flight.

———

I visualize an eagle as it soars through the air, high above the earth's surface. Observing this majestic bird in flight, I can't help wishing I was up there, gliding so smoothly, so effortlessly, weightless and free. I bring my attention closer to her in order to get a feel for what flying is all about, and I find myself so close that I can hear and see her feathers being buffeted by the wind. I notice her eyes twitching left and right as she plots her course. I see how by tilting her wings one way, her flight path is immediately altered in that direction before leveling out again. I turn my attention back to her eyes and move in even closer, so close now that in the next instant I find myself behind those very eyes. I am inside this eagle, and it is me looking down onto the world from up above. I take a moment to accustom myself to my new body, feeling the position of my legs and my head, feeling my wings spanned out wide on either side of me as they catch the wind. Air rushes past me, caressing my face, washing over my body. I dip my left wing and feel my body tilt as I swoop left. Realigning my wings, I regain my even plane.

As I glance downward, I take in the vast greens and blues and browns that make up our beautiful earth. So high am I that, as I cast my eyes into the distance, I can pick up a faint curvature of the earth's horizon. I look back down, and the mere dipping of my head sends me plunging earthward. I direct my flight toward a patch of green forest below, restoring my horizontal flight path just above its lush canopy. Treetops swish by below me at electric speed, and a cacophony of forest sounds rises out of the trees and bush. I find myself racing over an array of every shade of green imaginable.

As I reach the end of the forest canopy, I see a canyon stretched out before me, its brown, rugged walls dropping down into a river below. I swoop into the canyon, down and across the face of its brown walls. As I tilt one way, then the other, I move to within inches of its rock face, marveling at the speed with which the rugged, dusty wall rushes by. I dip deeper into the canyon now, toward the river below, until I am flying within inches of its sparkling surface. I lower my talons, dipping them into the water as I race forward, feeling the splash of coolness on my claws. I notice myself being lifting into a state of bliss by the speed of it all, by the exhilaration and freedom of flight, by the sheer diversity and vibrancy of nature. With these wings, I can twist and turn as I wish. I can go anywhere, experience anything. I am a perfect instrument of flight, and I am totally present, truly alive. As I continue my path through the canyon and beyond, I take it all in, absorbing the thrill of being an eagle in full flight.

## Grounded by Gravity

Gravity, despite the inescapable influence it has on our lives, is invisible by design, meaning we tend to forget that it exists. However, by occasionally reminding ourselves of its simple, downward pull, we can include it in our meditations as a useful tool in helping our bodies settle nicely. It can ground us, too, enabling us to connect to the earth in a real way.

I seat myself comfortably—or lie down, if I wish—and become aware of a gentle downward pull. This is the call of gravity. I feel its force drawing me toward the earth, drawing me into the earth. I focus for a moment on this silent force and the feeling it exerts on my body, observing how my flow of energy is being pulled gently toward the earth's core. I free the muscles in my body, letting them become heavy, not resisting this downward pull in any way. I just let them hang loose, let them flow with gravity's pull. It's as though gravity is inviting me to feel the earth, to appreciate this great mass beneath me. I become aware of those contact points connecting me to the earth: my feet, the backs of my legs, my buttocks. I can feel how gravity is drawing my energy down through these parts of my body.

Taking a moment to appreciate the gentle charge of electricity that exists at these contact points, I detect a warm glow, a buzz of energy on each part of my body touching the earth's surface. I shift my focus to my body as a whole now, and I appreciate how relaxed, how comfortably heavy it is. I take a gentle, slow breath in, drawing air deep into my stomach. And as I breathe out, I allow my body to sink and settle further into the earth. I repeat this, inhaling and exhaling, letting gravity's force relax me more. Simple breathing, simple gravity. I become aware of the weight of my body pressing downward, descending more with every exhalation. *Ah*, my body feels so good in this released state.

I remain in this position, just enjoying the gentle downward force, enjoying the feeling of letting my body go. My muscles are loose, my mind calm. This is my time to enjoy my body and the earth in union. It's time for my body to recharge, taking as much benefit as it can from these moments of deep rest. I feel the comforting presence of the earth beneath me and the play of her gentle energy on my skin. As she lovingly pulls me downward, I take the fullness of this experience in, this sensation of gravity grounding me and connecting my body to the earth in a real way.

## Returning to Playfulness

Few things in life are as satisfying as a stroll across a meadow bathed in warm spring sunshine. With a little visualization, we can do just that—regardless of the season we may find ourselves in!

It's a warm spring day, and I allow the image of a rolling, lush meadow to enter my mind. My surrounds are bathed in golden sunshine, giving the greenery a gorgeous shimmer. I follow the contours of the meadow as they dip and rise in the distance, rolling endlessly on. I bring my attention back to where I am standing on this soft grass, and I notice that I'm barefoot.

I begin to walk, and I enjoy how the spongy grass massages the soles of my feet. I take time to appreciate how such a simple act as walking can offer such sensory pleasure. Every step I make activates a gorgeous tingling sensation in the soles of my feet, and this feeling reverberates up through my legs, into my core, invigorating my whole body. The ground is warm, the grass springy and fresh.

As I make contact with the earth with each step, that healthy buzz jets up through my legs and spills into my torso. I feel my face opening up in a gentle smile, and again I am drawn into the vastness of my surrounds, the open greenery of it all. I sense an immeasurable freedom here, and glancing within, I see that very freedom reflected in my heart. Like this vast field before me, my heart is open wide. Suddenly the thought of running across this meadow enters my mind, and before I know it, I have picked up my pace and am jogging, now dashing across the grass. An instant later, I am leaping through the air, a cool breeze streaming over my face as I take energy-infused bound after bound. I am engulfed by a deep sense of freedom. Childlike abandon washes through me as I soar across the meadow, embracing each lunge as I invite crisp oxygen and pure sunshine into my being. A feeling of blissful playfulness overwhelms me, filling my being with sparkle. My heart is bursting with joy as I dive through the air, each leap more energized, empowered, and free. The moment is rich, nature is beautiful, and life is radiant and full.

## Nurtured by Nature

By observing nature, we learn not only about our surrounds, but about our inner world, too. Nature can serve as a powerful reflection of the qualities we wish to reawaken or deepen in ourselves. By appreciating the stillness in a tree, for example, or the purity in a river, we automatically emerge those very qualities in ourselves.

Let's manifest some of nature's beauty within us as we listen to her fullness, letting her guide us toward growth.

I become aware of my surrounds, of nature in all her flourishing beauty. Everything shines with some special quality. The trees, the plants, the flowers, and the grass all sparkle with life. Simply by observing nature, by opening my heart to the environment, I recognize her sacred essence. I let my vision settle on a tree, and I become aware of how still it is, how silently it stands. It simply exists, giving off its own vital energy in such an unassuming way. There may be a breeze ruffling its leaves or wind swaying its branches, but the tree remains stable, staying deeply rooted in the earth.

As I observe this tree and its calmness, its stability, I become aware of a similar stability existing in me. I am like this tree, rooted and connected to the earth. I turn my attention to where my feet make contact with the ground, feeling the solid presence of the earth below me. I sense her strength. I can draw on this strength, too. I can take her energy in. And as I do so, as I quietly receive the earth's energy through my feet, I feel an inner strength burgeoning within, a strength that brings stability and calm. Here, observing my surrounds from the stillness of my inner world, the trees, the plants, and the fields all respond with their own calm. My surrounds seem so much more still from my own perspective of stillness. Everything seems so much more peaceful from my position of peace.

I become aware of that beautiful tree again, rooted so deeply in the earth, and take the memory of its stability and strength with me into the day. As I interact with others, as I conduct my daily affairs, I remember that tree, tall and strong, stable and still. With that deep, grounding power in me, I watch as my day unfolds in a gentle, calm way.

## Diving into a Deepwater Cleanse

*Water.* Isn't there something perfectly magical about it? How rejuvenated we feel after a crisp swim in the ocean. Even the simple act of gazing out over a body of water can do wonders for our mood, reviving us and laying a foundation of peace within. Let's give ourselves over to the serenity of water, allowing its expansiveness to guide us into a deep meditation.

In my world within, I see a lake spread out before me. I take a moment to appreciate its vastness. The surface of the lake is flat and still, reflecting an array of colors: the blues of the sky, the greens of the surrounding forest, and the browns of distant mountains.

As I begin walking toward this lake, I become aware of a deep energy coming from this immense body of water, a distinct atmosphere that grows tangibly stronger as I approach it. Perhaps it's a calming energy that I feel, or one of silence, purity, or strength. The closer I come to the lake, the richer this energy feels, almost palpable now. I remove my shoes and walk onto its bank, feeling the soft sand under my feet, now the warm slosh of mud between my toes. The mud massages the soles of my feet as I walk.

I move gently into the shallow water, ankle-deep now, and the water's coolness seeps into my legs, awakening something bright in me. And deeper in I go, up to my calves, my knees, my hips, my stomach—all the way up to my chest. I become aware of the dance of the cool water over my skin, and I focus on this feeling, on the freshness it brings as the lake's water goes about cleaning and purifying the different parts of my body.

I now tilt my head back and lift and straighten my legs so that I am lying on my back. Here, floating effortlessly on the lake's surface, I peer up at the blue sky and embrace the tremendous openness up there. My vision relaxes as it gazes into the blue vastness above. With nothing to lock onto, my eyes just wander about, free. I bring my attention back to my body and feel the water continuing its gentle massage as it laps up against my skin, as it swirls around me. The water seems to carry with it a special energy, and I open myself up to this energy, absorbing it through the expanse of my skin.

I now roll over onto my stomach and ready myself to dive into the still waters below. I take a deep breath, and keeping my eyes open, down I go into the cool waters below. Crisp water sweeps across my face and scalp, invigorating me, awakening an alertness of mind. In this heightened state, I look around and observe the enormity of the lake's underwater expanse, its crystal underbelly. Everything shimmers with a turquoise light. I take a moment to appreciate this magic, watery world that stretches out far into the distance.

Now, as I kick off and glide forward through the water's revitalizing coolness, I again notice how spotless my body feels and how lucid my mind is. Here, within the lake's embrace, I feel a deep connection to its contents, to the

cleansing nature of the water streaming over me, continuing to enrich my body and purify my mind.

## Offering My Heart to Nature

We've all had an experience of being overwhelmed by the beauty
of nature. A common reaction to this is a desire to somehow
express gratitude toward the earth. One way to do so is via a simple, slow bow; this, done with feeling, conveys respect and thanks
while bringing us into the present, enhancing our appreciation of
nature all the more.

In the following exercise, we do just that, opening our hearts
up wide and offering thanks to our natural environment.

I find myself in a natural setting—or in the passenger seat of
a car, bus, or train passing through nature. I take a moment
to observe the beauty of my surrounds, be it a forest, a
beach, a meadow, or even my very own garden. Looking
deeply into the richness of all the growth happening—in the
grass, the flowers, the shrubs, the trees—I feel a distinct life
force emanating from nature.

As I get a more acute sense of this energy, of the vitality and purity sprouting so unconditionally from nature
without expecting anything in return, I feel I want to recip-
rocate. I want to somehow thank nature for her tireless
beauty she so steadfastly emits. So, with nature's splendor
imprinted in my mind, I close my eyes and continue to feel
her luminous beauty radiating out around me. I feel her

innate vibration, and it touches something deep inside me. Yes; I wish to offer gratitude for all her gentle splendor.

Slowly, very slowly, I begin to tilt my head forward in a reverent bow, all the while aware of nature's force existing like a soft mist around me. She is alive, her vibration constant, powerful. I continue my slow bow, holding on to my connection with nature, feeling her energy. If it's a river that's in front of me, I feel this very river flowing through me, calming me. If it's a breeze, I feel the breeze fluttering against my skin, cooling me. If it's a mountain, I feel the mountain's force inside me, stabilizing me. If it's an ocean, I feel her power rumbling inside me, strengthening me. If it's a forest, I feel her vitality, energizing me. If it's an animal, I feel her alertness, awakening me. Nature's force is not just around me, but inside me. I bathe in her aura, touching her sacred flow. We exist together. And as I complete my forward bow, I feel the energy of appreciation flowing from my heart, outward into nature. I feel myself giving, thanking, loving—and my love is a spring, streaming outward. I remain gently bowed over for as long as I wish, simply appreciating nature's beauty while offering love.

Finally, when I am ready, I straighten up slowly and open my eyes. Raising my hands, palms facing outward to nature, I feel that same love flowing out through my hands toward her. Simultaneously, I feel nature's giving force. I feel her essence coming my way. As I inhale, my palms change from giving to receiving, and I take nature's energy in. I accept her fullness, her purity.

As I exhale again, I return to giving, freeing my love and letting it flow out through my palms into nature. I am in a divine exchange with nature, her energy flowing into me, my energy flowing out to her. In this consecrated moment of togetherness, my breath and hers are in harmony. We are divinely connected, existing in a warm cycle of giving and receiving. We are touching and being touched by each other's energy, by each other's fullness, by each other's love.

## Opening Up to Nature's Voice

The practice of sitting quietly and listening to nature as a form of meditation has been performed throughout time, whether consciously or unconsciously. It invites a calming yet uplifting experience as we get in touch with nature's peace and power. The more we engage with nature in this way, the more we uncover her intrinsic beauty.

Focusing on nature can also open us up to universal messages. When we consciously listen to the voice of nature—with that voice being her sounds, her colors, her shapes, her atmosphere, her life force—we move from a state of incessant thought production to a quieter, more receptive state. The immediate result is inner silence, and in the heightened state of awareness this silence brings, we may find ourselves drawn to something in our surrounds—a plant, tree or bird, or even the wind or sky. If we're very still and in tune with the moment, an insect or animal may even trust us enough to settle beside us. Dragonflies seem especially unthreatened by humans, often perfectly at home using our bodies as landing pads!

Once we've determined which part of our environment is vying for our attention, we can dive deeper in, entering a sacred communion with that very element. By listening carefully and opening up to nature's vibration in this way, we may well receive a subtle message from the universe. The universe is, after all, geared to assist us on so many levels and in so many subtle ways.

As we listen to nature, the environment becomes our teacher. First, though, we need to become quiet and listen for her gentle whisper. Because within that whisper is a world of wisdom designed solely for those who take the time to listen carefully.

Let's open up our hearts and ears and catch that universal wisdom embedded in nature's purr.

———

I sit very quietly in nature, allowing my senses to become alert. I am alive to my surrounds, very present, very conscious of all that is happening in front of me. I exist, as does nature around me. And in my quiet, receptive state, I sense how my surrounds are coming to life. Everything looks and feels so fresh, so full, the environment bursting with life. I tune in to the sound of nature—maybe the rustling of her leaves, or the whistle of her breeze, or the buzz of insects and chatter of birds. I open up to these sounds, allowing them to fill my being. As they enter me, nature enters me.

All I am doing is sitting quietly and inviting nature and her sounds inward. As the fullness of nature flows into me, as her atmosphere permeates my being, I become acutely aware of all her colors, her shapes, her textures. I let my eyes drift across my surrounds until something specific beckons me, vies for my attention, calls me toward itself. It may be a tree, a plant, an animal. Whatever it is, I find it, and I focus on it. This is my message medium. I silently ask it,

"Do you wish to tell me something? What is the universe saying to me through you?"

I wait silently, patiently, all the while opening myself for a response. Opening up my heart, my world, my consciousness.

"What can you pass on to me that I need to know?"

I listen carefully, giving nature a chance to offer me a sliver of universal wisdom. I am fully receptive, simply absorbing the mood of my environment and waiting for the response I know will come. I may feel a wave being emitted of some beautiful quality—perhaps strength, or love, or stillness. Or maybe a bright thought simply flashes up in my mind. I wait for as long as I need to, patiently enjoying this quiet time alone, simply listening to nature. And when my message comes, I accept it gratefully. Having received my message, I take several moments to reflect on it, to savor it, to feel it in my heart. And now, I say my own silent prayer to nature, thanking her for showing me her beauty and sharing her wisdom with me.

## Filling Up with Earth's Breath

It's no wonder that the ancient healing practice of barefoot walking in nature is enjoying a recent resurgence. The earth, after all, exudes a vital energy that can both ground and energize us—especially when done without the encumbering nature of shoes! Plants and trees do this all the time, of course, sinking their roots into the earth and drawing from her energy pool. Indeed, every creature on this planet, in some way, relies on the earth's energy, without which we'd all quickly become extinct.

But what exactly is this vital force the earth so silently emits? Can we really tune in and use it to nurture and empower us? Let's find out for ourselves as we explore our relationship with the earth by listening to and feeling her mysterious forces.

———

Sitting down in nature, I become aware of my surrounds. I start by taking in my immediate vicinity: the colors, the shapes, the atmosphere. I listen to the sounds nature emits via her creaks, her whispers, her songs. I sit back and let these sounds encircle me, touch me, massage me. And now I go deeper, to beyond these sounds, to something more fundamental and basic. I tune in to nature's hum existing beneath all the sounds. I listen to the earth's life-giving pulse, to her heartbeat, to her deep murmur.

This sound of the earth's energy may reveal itself to me in any number of ways. In whichever form I experience it, I tune in to it. I feel it—that raw, instinctive energy rising from somewhere deep below, surfacing right beneath me. I open my body to this vibration, to this pulse that flows up from the earth's depths. This is her life force, her breath, and I let her in. I feel waves of earth energy flowing into me, into my body, into my heart, and I absorb them. I am being filled by nature's clean vibration, becoming full with her potency. And now, very gradually, I imagine these waves of energy to be the earth's exhalations.

As she breathes out, her forces enter me. I catch the fullness of these forces, soaking them up and making them part of me. Now, as the earth inhales a deep, long in-breath lasting twenty seconds and more, I feel a soothing pull, a gentle force drawing me toward her center. I feel myself being taken into her warmth, into her womb, in one long, gentle, soothing pull. I simply let go, drifting alongside that force as it takes me into her depths. And so it is that I find myself within the earth. Being here, I can get a real sense of her strength. And still her inhalation continues, drawing me deeper in, until I am right at her center. I rest here within her powerful core and give myself a moment to contemplate her energy, to open myself up even more to it, to experience it more vividly. Here, at the heart of the earth, I begin to understand the immensity of it all. And as she exhales again, I feel all that raw, vital energy streaming straight into me. Her force flows in, filling me, lifting me.

I take as long as I wish, here at the center of the earth, to move with her breath, to restore my own vital life force by tapping into hers. And when I am ready, I rise slowly back to the surface and become aware of my surrounds again, of the effervescent beauty in nature. I feel an even deeper connection with my environment now, knowing it is—like me—breathing that same essential earth energy I was seated beside, seated within, just moments before. I am a child of the earth, and I feel her deep breath, slowly drawing in, slowly pushing out.

## Celebrating the Sanctity of Fruit

Fruit, besides being deliciously healthy, is revered for its purity; just think how frequently it's used in religious ceremonies as a kind of spiritual offering. Indeed, such is the fullness of fruit's beauty that artists ceaselessly attempt to capture its essence on canvas via still lifes.

Let's pay tribute to nature's finest bounty as we conduct a small ceremony of our own before indulging in fruit's sweet substance.

I hold a piece of fruit gently between my hands, my palms encircling it. I feel its skin touching mine and become conscious of its weight, of the fullness it carries within. Simply by holding this fruit, I already sense the profound healing potential it contains within. I reflect for a moment on all that fruit offers: its health-giving properties, its vitality, its clean vibration, its depth of taste. I wish to celebrate, to fully appreciate the true value of this beautiful element of nature. And so, with closed eyes, I raise the fruit very slowly, very respectfully, until it is just in front of my forehead. And as I do so—in a gesture of gratitude—I bow my head gently to meet it.

I hold this position, head bowed with the fruit inches away from my forehead, and become aware of my own vital energy, located like a powerful light behind my eyes. I observe as this energy, indeed the light of my soul, filters out, encircling and embracing the fruit, now entering it. I continue directing my energy toward the fruit, purifying it further, filling it more with sacred substance. I let the fruit gently touch my forehead now and feel its energy against my skin. And still I release my spiritual energy, filling the fruit with even more potential, more power. Our two energies are merged, my warmth with its warmth. My fullness with its fullness.

And now, finally, I lower the fruit to my lips, and slowly, reverently, I take a bite. I accept its wholeness, its freshness into my mouth. As I begin to chew, I do so very consciously, aware of the richness of its taste, of its nutrient-dense nature, of its vibrant juices. And as I swallow, I feel its energy enter me. I feel it filling me, pleasing me, healing me as its life force merges with mine. It is now an essential part of me, and I feel its glow deep within, offering me sustenance and health.

## Embracing the Energy of Rain

Rainy days are quick to receive a bad rap, with them frequently being labeled "bad weather." How unfair! Not only does rain nourish the earth, it creates a soft atmosphere, too, promoting self-reflection. What's more, it gifts us an opportunity to engage in indoor chores we might otherwise have neglected. And then there's summer rain … now *that* is something to treasure. What's more refreshing, after all, than a downpour on a hot, steamy day!

In the following visualization exercise, we embrace the wonder of rain and allow it to guide us toward inspiration and renewal.

———

With eyes closed, I tilt my head gently back and imagine myself peering up at the sky. Up above, storm clouds gather. They are dark and burly, full and ready, unmistakably on the verge of eruption. It's a warm day, and both the earth and I are thirsty for the promise these clouds offer. While observing the sky and its imminent downpour, I feel the tiniest splash on my forehead. The first drop has fallen!

I follow this droplet as it rolls down my face, deliciously cool and ticklish. It moves over my chin before finally falling off me. A second drop splashes onto my face now, a soft, refreshing burst of water. Now a third drop, and before I know it, it has begun to drizzle. Dozens of droplets pitter-patter my face. How fresh they feel! How soothing this rain is as it gently massages my skin, as it flows down my face, down my neck, down my body. How cleansing it is, this rain falling from the pure skies above, washing over my body in small, dancing rivulets. I observe one such stream on my face and follow it as it snakes its way down my body, leaving a tingling sensation in its path.

Observing the entirety of my body, I realize this is but one of a multitude of waterways flowing over me, each one leaving their tingling imprint, each one's flow like a soft, cool, healing massage. I now shift my focus to above my body, to the sky, observing the dark underbelly of the clouds. I can see the rain as it discharges from each cloud, and I watch the thousands of droplets tumble down toward me, exploding as they land on me.

The more I concentrate on the falling rain, the slower it seems to fall, until it's all in slow motion ... rain falling ever so gradually, so peacefully from above. I focus on an individual droplet now, floating earthward, and I see the fullness of its beauty, this little dome of water bulging and contracting as it falls. It resembles a water-filled balloon, its skin shifting as it struggles to hold its energy-laden contents within. This soft, sparkling globule of water catches and reflects light, a jewel descending from above. And it falls, falls, falls, coming closer and closer to my face. Splash! It bursts on my forehead, sending a ripple of refreshing energy through my skin, inward, straight into my core, dousing me with its purity, with its life giving vibration. And the slow-falling rain continues to fall, a legion of drops tumbling down before exploding on my skin, each one sending fresh energy inward.

My body welcomes each droplet, embracing it, reaching out to it. I absorb the vigor of each one of these waterdrops spilling down onto me, accepting their healing force into me. My mouth is wide open now, and I catch the rain on my tongue. As delicate bursts of crisp water plummet into my mouth, I swallow, and I feel a river of rain flowing down my throat. Its coolness finds its way deep into my body, filling me with its essence. And still the rain falls, into my mouth, onto my skin. I surrender to its renewing energy, my entire being welcoming this rain from above. I give myself entirely over to the invigorating showers descending from the skies above, taking their fullness and vibrancy deeply in.

# Chapter 8
# Heaven

Eden, Paradise, Elysium, Shangri-La, Utopia, Zion—indeed, Heaven! We've all heard incredible tales about this promised land, but does it even exist, and if so, where? What does it look like—or, more importantly, what does it *feel* like?

Heaven has been described as that land of perfection, its inhabitants pure and vibrant and flowing with love. Interactions with others are deep and meaningful, and bliss is second nature. Everyone's focus is squarely on the present—and a beautiful present, at that—meaning life is full and wondrous.

Sound vaguely appealing? Sure it does! Except for the fact that it's always describing a future world—the *promised* land. That doesn't sound right. Why should we have to wait, and wait some more, to live a life bursting with vibrancy and love? Shouldn't our present reflect at least some of that immaculate beauty?

It certainly should! And that's why, instead of longing for some distant paradise, we need to bring a piece of it right here, onto our planet, into our life, into this moment. By keeping our focus solely on the present, we can give ourselves the experience that, right now, everything within us *is* beautiful—heck, maybe even perfect. And when our inner worlds become filled with beauty, the outside world has a wonderful way of automatically reflecting some, if not all, of that beauty.

Let's stop dreaming about heaven and start living it, now.

## Placing Heaven in My Heart

Our experience of this very moment in time is fundamental to our happiness. That's why it's the *present* that requires our attention. And so, in order to invite abundance and joy into our lives, we need to remind ourselves that, right now, there is nowhere else we'd rather be. This place, this situation, this *second* we find ourselves in, is perfect.

By developing a wholesome relationship with the present, we place heaven squarely in our hearts and bring paradise to earth. That *is* where it belongs, after all.

⁓

Sitting here, I reflect on simple pleasures. I am seated comfortably in this chair, breathing easily. And this very act of being alive—of having the awareness that, right now, I exist, I feel, I think—this alone brings comfort and contentment. There need be nothing complicated about appreciating the present. Simply sitting here, breathing in and out as I experience life can be perfectly gratifying.

I take some time now to reflect on other joys of mine— perhaps my home that contains so many things I am thankful for, or my beautiful family and friends, or the deep, practical wisdom I have gained from a life filled with so many varied experiences. Yes; my reality is truly filled with abundance. I'd surely not trade places with anyone in the world. I am my own being, exquisitely molded through a life where not a single day has unfolded identically to another. The place I find myself in right now is absolutely accurate. It is exactly where I ought to be. I have brought myself here through that myriad of experiences, through my countless actions, through my interactions with others. I am in the perfect place, physically, emotionally, spiritually.

All the issues I dealt with in the past were opportunities to learn and gain wisdom, to grow into this precise version of me. With every passing moment, I was able to understand more about how to live life, about how to interact with myself and others. This is the being I have become. And I love that being. I love the me that has surfaced from the sum of all I've been through. I take a moment to feel this love, this deep affection for the being that is me. I look within, into the space of my heart, and I offer myself the warm embrace of love. I send this beautiful feeling inward. My love is full, and it brightens my interior.

Now, with one slow, deep in- and out-breath, I open my heart up wide. And I let the love in my heart roll out. I set love free, letting it do what it ought to: flow naturally and abundantly through the entirety of my being. And as this love circulates within me, as it saturates every part of my being, I feel every inner blockage being cleared. This stream of warm energy coursing through me frees up the spaces within, lighting up my inner world. And with all this incredible warmth right here inside me, with this current of love coursing through me, I realize that, yes, this moment is heaven. I hold paradise inside my heart, inside my being. This moment, this feeling is what perfect life is all about. This is what is meant by heaven. With an inner world replete with happiness and light, I walk forward, feeling the beautiful resonance of love within.

## Examining the Spiritual Experience

Describing spirituality—or more specifically, a spiritual experience—can be challenging, to say the least. In a vague kind of way, we might say, "It's a trip to another dimension."

The first response to that might be something to the tune of, "Oh, you're just a big hippie!" followed by a more serious inquiry: "So what is this *other dimension*? What does it feel like to be there?"

In the following meditation, we offer ourselves a firsthand glimpse of this higher, mystical world—a.k.a. the Other Dimension.

———

I take several deep, slow breaths. With each in-breath, gently drawing air in through my nose, I imagine it's light I'm breathing in. With each out-breath, as I push air out through my mouth, I allow my body to become empty. Inhaling, I breathe in light and become brighter. Exhaling, I empty my body, letting go as I free myself into the feeling of openness. I feel weightless now, my body replete with light alone.

I take a moment to observe my mind and conduct the same exercise here, breathing light into my mind, exhaling and emptying my mind. My mind, too, becomes unburdened and free. And now, looking into my body, into my mind, into everything that exists inside me, I see a clean environment radiant with light. And as I peer into that light, I acknowledge that I am staring straight into the spiritual dimension.

Within this light inside me, I inherently know there is something of the mystical within it—that within its atmosphere, the impossible can become possible. I contemplate the immensity of this reality for a moment: within me, I carry a dimension of spirit. And gazing into this very dimension, into my light, I wonder about this light's original home, about the totality of the spiritual world existing in another dimension. I'd like to discover what that vast dimension feels like, possibly even what it looks like. As a being of light myself, it goes without saying that I can, whenever I wish, take that journey to explore my original home of light. Right now, I choose to do that by letting go, and simply letting the experience happen.

I allow myself to drift upward, to that plane made up entirely of spiritual light. Before I know it, I find myself removed from my body, detached from the physical, in a space surrounded by soft light. I have stepped into the world of clean, pure, angelic light. I observe my surrounds and inspect the light to see what it holds within its misty beauty. I peer into its softly lit expanse to discover for myself the qualities it houses in its radiance, to explore its very essence. I can feel a distinct vibration within the light, an atmosphere. Maybe I sense something powerful, peaceful, or silent. Maybe it's overflowing with love or rich with magic. As I continue to examine and feel my surrounds, I take note of what I see in front of me. Maybe there's nothing but infinite, open space, lit up in all directions. Or a myriad of starlike souls floating brightly, shining vibrantly. It may be that I see angels communicating silently with one another.

Whatever it is I witness up here, in this higher world, I take it all in. I absorb its beautiful vibration and its gentle landscape. I now focus on any sounds I may hear. Is there a silent hush? Or a slow, deep, transformative Om? Are there gentle voices, or perhaps even angelic singing accompanied by the soothing plucking of a harp? I fill myself with the sounds of my surrounds, whatever they may be. I take them in, let them enter and become part of me.

I now direct my attention within to observe my own inner world as I exist in this spiritual world. How am I feeling? Am I weightless? Do I feel like I am floating, unburdened by physicality and utterly free? Do I feel a sense of eternity, of having no beginning and no end, just a continuous flow? Do I feel unlimited or even enlightened? What qualities have emerged in me? Maybe peace, contentment, love, or purity. One thing is for certain: I feel at home here. I resonate with all that is happening around me. I am perfectly comfortable in this space. This is, after all, my original home.

I take a moment to reflect on what I look like up here. Am I transparent, almost invisible? Or am I composed simply of light? Am I like a tiny star, or a great sun? If so, what is the color of my glow? Am I an angel, sparkling with light?

I take as much time as I need to experience all aspects of this higher dimension—the sounds, the sights, the atmosphere—while observing my inner world as it exists up here, too. With a sense of timeless patience, I allow myself to develop a deep understanding of my spiritual home. I simply rest here, observing and experiencing this sacred space as well as my state of being in this space. On this plane of light, everything is effortless. Feelings of the highest, most perfect kind are possible and natural. I let those feelings emerge in me, let them express themselves in their perfect form. Sitting here, I let go, freeing myself into the experience of spirituality. I exist in a state of pure being, in a world of pure light. Everything is as it should be. The world is at peace, and within, I am perfectly full.

# Chapter 9
## Soul

"Who am I?" is surely the simplest yet deepest question known to mankind. It's also possibly the question no book has the answer to, thus begging the next question: "Where can we go to find the answer?"

To our very own hearts, of course! Surely that's where this *I* is seated, right? We need to look within, gazing straight into the energy of the self, and wallow in the experience that follows. It's through this experience—of listening to our own life vigor—that answers about our true identity are revealed.

This conscious energy within—the *I*—is often referred to as the soul. Many experience it as inner light. Yet this is no ordinary light; it's dynamic, virtuous, creative light. It's light that is *alive*. And once we tune in to the soul's multifaceted vibration, its intelligence, we begin to awaken our true spiritual potential, and we can explore ways to utilize this power.

In looking for this energy of the soul, some use visualization, at least initially, to "see" the soul—that brilliant inner light. And once sighted, the experience of truly feeling it as the seat from which consciousness and life emerge comes naturally. In this way—by seeing then feeling the soul—we effortlessly usher in a spiritual experience. And once this practice becomes a habit—going within and reconnecting with our original, primary energy source—we can access meditative states on a whim. We can move through life constantly connected to spirit, affording us an automatic foundation of peace and gentle power.

The trick, though, is to *remember* to look within and to listen for that soft, spiritual hum. Let's do that now, leaving behind the multitudinous writings on the subject of *soul*, and head off on our own quest to discover what lies within.

## Getting Acquainted with the Soul

Some experience the soul as a spark of light, small yet powerful, located just behind the eyes—indeed, as the third eye. Maybe the soul is just that: intelligent light existing at the center of our mind, always shining, always conscious; an energy that never goes flat, giving us the gift of eternal life. And eternity … that's a long time!

Now, imagine for a moment we could tap into an *eternally* intelligent energy source and wallow in its power, whenever and for as long as we wished. Imagine we could drink, and drink again, from its endless fountain. What if, for just one minute—one *focused* minute—we could bathe in the splendor of our very own spiritual light? What miraculous effect might that have on us?

Of course, through meditation, we can do precisely this. The experience of our own spirituality, our own inner perfection, that meeting with *self*, is perfectly accessible to us—right now, if we wish. And when we surface after having touched our eternal self, after renewing that divine innermost connection, wouldn't we be a little—dare I say—enlightened?

Let's dive deep within, journeying to the core of our being as we explore the beauty of our inner light. Let's see what the *I* at the center of our being is all about.

———

I rest my entire body, just letting it be. It is comfortable and relaxed. Settled. Still. And in this peaceful state, I dive within. I go beneath my skin, on a mission to find that spark of life existing at the center of my being. Here, deep inside my body, I am on a journey to discover, firsthand, what it is that keeps me thinking, feeling, moving. I wish to find the very source of my awareness, that spark allowing me to be conscious of this moment, that spark enabling me to experience the world as it exists around me.

Seated within, I become an observer, examining my inner environment, quietly looking across all that exists here. I watch for any movement, any vibration, any energy. I listen for signs of life—perhaps a sound or a feeling related to being alive. And as I do so, as I simply sit and listen, I am giving the soul a platform to reveal itself, to allow me to see my own essence, to meet the real me.

Waiting patiently, I watch for that pulse of life—because something will reveal itself, I know. I may start to sense a distinct, concentrated energy or a vibration in a specific part of my body. Or maybe a flicker of light reveals itself, bright and clear. Or an empty, silent, peaceful space may simply open up within. Whatever it is, when this life force does emerge, I take note of how it feels. What energy is it giving off? I take several moments to get a sense of the atmosphere it exudes. And now I approach it, moving toward its source. I wish to discover its exact position, its dimensions, its substance. I go closer to this focal point of power within, closer and closer, until I am right beside it. And still closer I go, deeper and deeper in. I am inside it now—inside the very essence of me, the soul—resting at the center of my being. This is the true me beneath all the physicality. This is the me beyond my bodily costume, beyond the roles I play, beyond my nationality, beyond my likes and dislikes.

I feel the energy of the soul welling up around me, surfacing from this deep inner space that is me. I simply let go to it and enjoy the presence of my own life force, my very own hum of vitality. I inspect the energy I am emitting and notice how clean it is, how constant and alive it is. I bathe in my own glow as I radiate outward. This vibrancy—I, the soul, emitting living energy—is such a natural feeling, yet the experience is so deep. Here I am, seated within the center of my truth. Everything I am is within this point of energy, this spiritual space. I am clear, concentrated power. I am this, forever. And by knowing my roots, by understanding and experiencing the essence of who I am, I can draw strength and wisdom.

Here, spending time with the real me—the spiritual me existing at my center—I get a sense of my body and how it surrounds me. I become an observer of this body. I become an observer of the world, too, looking out through these eyes and picking up on any movement in my surrounds. A feeling of detachment comes over me, of being comfortably separated from all the noise of distracting emotion and activity. And despite my detachment, I feel love for my body and the world. Seated here within, I can appreciate the beauty of all that surrounds me without disruption. I can appreciate all that bustle without judgment. I can simply enjoy and love all.

When I am ready, I return to the surface, merging back into this body and the world around me. Even as I do so, I feel the spark of life within, continuing its shine. I remain conscious of the inner light that is me. And here, back in the physical realm, having experiential knowledge of who I am, I can reconnect to my power source at any time. All it takes is a single intentional thought to journey within, to see, touch, and feel my light. I can, at any time, dive deep within, entering my inner power and filling myself up with the purity of spirit. And when I am filled with spirit, life's journey becomes so much easier, so much fuller.

With my connection to divinity restored, my strength renewed, and my focus sharpened, life becomes more meaningful. I am in touch with authentic beauty, original wisdom, eternal truth. And as I move forward into the day, connected firmly to my inner spark, the world of spirit continues to nourish me every step of the way.

## Finding My Center

In attempting to unravel the mysteries of the universe, many turn to spirituality to find answers. Spirituality is a colorful pursuit indeed, offering us an untold number of different paths to explore truth. Yet as varied as the methods may be, a common thread throughout is the inquiry about the self: Who am I? What is consciousness? Where is the seat of life?

Many believe this living energy that we are, commonly referred to as the soul, is located behind the eyes, while others claim it resides in our hearts. Some believe it to be everywhere, or nowhere, or in a place impossible to define.

Whatever it is we've been told, it's personal experience that has the final say. That's what meditation is all about, after all: learning about the self via our own intimate experience.

Let's initiate that very experience as we journey within in search of our spiritual spark.

———

In this moment, I have awareness; that much is certain. I am aware that life exists around me. And I am aware of the life within. But this life force that I can feel right now, this conscious energy … where exactly is it surfacing from? Where is the origin of this inner spark of consciousness enabling me to experience life? To answer this question, I need to venture within. And so, sitting here, I allow myself to become quiet. I let my body settle into stillness. With each breath, I become more still, more settled.

Now, by gazing to the world within, I direct my energy inward. I observe my inner reality. There is life in here; that much I know. I know it because I can feel it—that vibrant, tangible energy of life. I focus on this inner vitality allowing me to be conscious, enabling awareness of this moment, of my body, of my existence. It's clear that yes, I am here, surrounded by this physical world.

So where is this *I*, this consciousness that knows all this? I listen very carefully to what's happening within, to that pulse telling me that I exist, that I am here. It may be that I feel the sensation of life in a specific location. Or I may sense a wide-ranging energy being emitted from various parts of my being. If this is the case, I simply observe the totality of this energy and wait for its source to reveal itself. Every living being surely has a source, after all—a pinpoint from which life emerges. And when I sense the origin of my life force, I move toward it. I simply go there, dropping into its midst, into this space in my body that signals life. It's from here, inside this space, that life sprouts. I nestle myself deep within, in the center of this spark of life. I am now seated at the heart of my being, resting at the point from which my life force emerges. This burgeoning energy is me. I am this conscious spark, and it's from this point of consciousness that I control my thoughts, my feelings. Surrounded by my body, I control my movements, too.

Perched here in my control tower, I feel a profound comfort rising in me, a sense of warmth and safety. I am in a state of perfect balance, and from here, I operate my world. I create my thoughts, my feelings. From here, I pilot this vehicle of my body. I am able to move it with calmness, with confidence.

I take a moment to observe the outside world—from this space within—through these eyes. Everything is so serene from this secure vantage point. I truly am in control of my life. I am the master of my own world, and I move forward with conviction. I embrace life, holding on to the awareness of my awakened spirit within. With every step I take, I feel the stirring influence of my inner light flowing outward into my movements, into my life.

## Examining My Inner Om

Meditation sensitizes us to our inner and outer environments, allowing us to pick up on subtleties we might otherwise miss. And one such subtlety—perhaps the subtlest of them all—is that of the soul embedded deep within. Meditation gives us that power of self-observation—of going within and listening to and seeing our inner world, of discovering our spirit. We deepen our understanding of ourselves and our potential as we probe the reservoir of wisdom and power housed in the soul.

Let's reconnect with our unique energy, giving ourselves that firm reminder of the dazzling heights we're capable of as spiritual beings.

—

Seated here, I reflect on that perennial question: "Who am I?" What is this inner energy I feel that enables awareness of being right here, right now? Indeed, who is the conscious being who is asking this very question? As I reflect on my existence, on the energy giving life to me, I find my vision naturally drawn inward. And as I go within, I take a moment to get a feel for my inner environment. What energy is running through me? What is this vibration of life that buzzes within? What does it feel like? And this vibration I feel, is this not the very *I* I'm inquiring about? Is this not the soul that I am feeling? And if so, where is it located? Where is my center, the origin of my spiritual energy? Would it surely not lie at the very source of my consciousness?

Let me find that area, that point from where my consciousness emerges. Let me go to that spark of life telling me that I exist right now. I look deep within, and there it is. I feel it, maybe even see it: my life force glowing like a star at the center of my being. It is still, yet vibrant. Soft, yet powerful. I focus for a moment on its light and on the energy it emits. This spark is none other than me, and its vibration is my energy, my life force, emerging from me. I am seeing myself right now. I am looking into the being that is me, manifested as a spark of concentrated light.

I take note of how my energy surfaces and spreads outward in the form of light and conclude that I shine in a very special way. I look deeply into this light now, with the aim to understand its substance more profoundly. I see that it's composed of thousands of spiritual photons—tiny, perfect particles of light flowing outward in a concentric arc around me. I watch in fascination as these particles of light radiate out from the center of my being—myriads of little, dazzling lights. I now imagine these particles of light to be miniature, tactile Oms, each one carrying a sacred vibration. And I observe as I, this glowing soul within, emit a never-ending stream of tiny yet powerful Oms.

These vibrations, these pockets of purring light, caress me as they flow from my center through all parts of my body. Into my torso they go, down my legs and arms, up my neck, and into my head. I watch as these particles of Om work their way through me, and I feel their power. I feel the comforting effect of this smooth river of energy winding its way through me. I allow each individual Om making up this lively current to massage me internally, to fill my entire body, to vibrate its healing light into me. I am being energized by my own living, pulsing light, cleansed by my own dynamic life force. I, the soul, continue my out-pouring of light, and my flow is satiated with the sound of Om. This stream of pulsing light, this river of Om flows through me, filling and cleaning me while injecting life.

## Fueling Myself with Light

When we feel lethargic or uninspired, purposeful action becomes difficult. What's needed is a surge of power to kick-start our enthusiasm, rekindle our positivity, and get us moving forward again.

Let's ignite that fire, now.

I sit quietly and summon my spiritual flame, my spark of energy within. In an instant, it reveals itself to me as a pin-prick of light at the center of my being. I observe it for a moment, this tiny inner spark, and I watch in wonder as it begins to grow in size and power. I feel it as a warm energy within now, expanding its influence, becoming stronger, pushing out more light.

Within this light, I sense a well of deep substance, of might and wisdom that can—and will—carry me forward in the right direction. All I need to do is surrender to my inner light, to its warm guidance and strength. By simply giving myself over to its influence, I will be directed to where I need to go. I need to just trust the light by placing it at the forefront of my consciousness, at the forefront of my actions. I need to simply let the light do the work and let its power move me. And I do just that: I position my glowing inner light at the center of my world, at the apex of my being, and I let it lead me. I let it take me forward. And as I proceed into today, I do so with the confidence that I am divinely guided. Surrendered to my inner light, I am carried forward safely and purposefully.

As I move in the presence of inner light, this very light flows into my actions, turning them into something special, something spiritual. Directed by the light, every action becomes accurate and easy, every movement graceful and fluid. I think less; I exist more. As I move forward, following my own light, my actions are powerful, and my life is vibrant and bright.

## Restoring the Balance Within

Success, however we may define it, is something we all strive toward—especially folk who read books on meditation! Success—or any other metric of a good life, be it health, wealth, or finding love—can of course be achieved physically, emotionally, mentally, and spiritually. By achieving a degree of success on each of these levels, we move toward a life of holistic health. Neglecting one at the expense of another, however, will inevitably leave us unfulfilled and in a state of imbalance. We could be the picture-perfect athlete yet find ourselves lacking maturity or a sense of stability; as a result, we'd be hard-pressed to find lasting happiness. Appreciating the intricate connectedness of these various dimensions and applying practices to reach a degree of fulfillment in each one will assist us in finding that happiness.

In order to meet our various needs on these four levels, we need to begin by acknowledging our success stories in each area; maybe our three-times-a-week jog in the park leads us toward physical health, an inspiring relationship with our partner contributes to our emotional health, and our daily self-reflection practice boosts our mental and spiritual health.

At the same time, we need to evaluate our shortcomings in each area. We may have an area of our diet we could improve on, or a toxic relationship we could eliminate, or a habit of putting off our quiet time until "tomorrow."

Let's start by doing a quick assessment of our physical health:

- What am I doing physically that I feel good about? My morning stretches? Not eating after 8:00 p.m.? Getting enough sleep?

- What am I doing that I'd be better off *not* doing? Smoking? Driving to the shops when I could cycle instead? Taking the elevator instead of the stairs?

- What am I *not* doing that I could be doing? Drinking water first thing in the morning? Making sure I'm getting thirty minutes of daily exercise? Eating a healthy dose of salad with my dinner?

The same questions can be asked of our emotional, mental, and spiritual practices. Reflecting in this way will nudge us toward a more balanced, holistic life as we pay attention to all areas of our existence.

Balance also exists on a deeper, unseen level. Let's check ourselves now:

"Am I feeling balanced within?"

It's a subtle feeling, this thing called balance. But with regular inward inspections, we can get accustomed to assessing our degree of internal balance and make corrections where necessary.

Right now, let's consciously invoke an experience of being centered within ourselves.

Start off by finding your midpoint and resting there, observing your position and surrounds. Once you feel you're more or less centered, make a few micro adjustments, shifting slightly this way or that way until a feeling of perfect balance emerges. This feels good, yes! That's right; sit back and enjoy this sensation of being perfectly centered within. Now watch as your internal blockages start to dissolve. Allow your inner environment to open up, facilitating an even, free flow of energy that restores and nurtures your inner world. *Ah*, now this is the beauty of balance!

Let's continue exploring this feeling of stabilizing ourselves in our center as we open up those inner pathways. Let's allow our river of life to flow naturally—the way all good rivers should!

⌣

I reflect for a moment on inner balance and what it means to me. Where is my center from which I can restore internal symmetry, allowing my energy to flow unobstructed and free? To find the answer, I simply go within. I find that pocket of warmth inside me from which life emerges. Once detected, I very naturally place myself in its center, settling comfortably inside my very own spring of life.

Here, centered in the seat of the soul, I notice how bright and strong this energy I am emitting is. I marvel at the soul's golden beacon of light that shines out from me. It's from here, inside this spark of inspiring energy that is me, that I operate my world. It's from here that I create thoughts, make decisions, and feel sensations. Within this living fountain of light is my mind, my consciousness, allowing me to experience my shimmer as it flows out from me in a vivid, intelligent glow. How good it feels to be so perfectly centered within. How calm everything is down here. I exist in a place of deep purity, of true power.

I now observe my body surrounding me, becoming acutely aware of the sensation of physicality shrouding me. This body is my temple, and I am seated within its beautiful domain. I let my purity, my power radiate outward into this temple. I let my light shine out in all directions at once from this center-point I am resting in. My inner glow streams outward in a symmetrical arc from soul to body, from spirituality into physicality.

This river of light, this essential flow, rolls unobstructed across my entire body, opening up all my inner pathways as it spills outward. It enters the farthest reaches of my body, cleaning me while encouraging me back toward perfect health. Centered within, I watch as this restoration, this return to harmony unfolds. I take a moment to appreciate that harmony, that feeling of balance across my entire being. I observe my free flow of energies in this open, clean environment of my inner world. I am warm light, sentient energy, and my vibration is sacred and pure.

## Funneling Light into Action

The soul can be described as living light fueled by its own inherent, eternal power. When we consciously access this power and bring it into our physical world, wonderful things start to happen.

Let's get a glimpse of this spiritual wonder within by intentionally placing ourselves at the center of the soul before initiating an action, then drawing on this pure inner energy. Let's see how focused, how meaningful, how *powerful* our activity becomes in the presence of spirit and decide for ourselves if divine action is all it's touted to be.

⸻

Sitting here, I observe my body. I become aware of how it's like a costume, surrounding the true life force within—that spark of spiritual light that is me. In order to touch, and enjoy, and draw from my spiritual center, I need to be beside that inner light. I need to feel it. So, I shift my awareness to within, and immediately sense a pulse of energy coming from deep inside. I move toward it, and the closer I get to my center, to my essence, the more vividly I feel that bright spark of life and its waves of pure, gentle power. I move closer still, and into the light I go.

I find myself deep within the very spark that is me, that primary energy of the soul. I am within my light, surrounded by my light. Here, at the center of my being, I can feel those waves of clean, spiritual energy I emit so consistently, so naturally. I focus on the feeling within these waves of energy as they emerge from me, as they flow through me. I sense their deep purity, their fullness. I could just sit here forever, appreciating my own vital inner life force that emerges and flows from the core of my being.

Now, very gently, I start to spread my light out into my body. And as my soft, shimmering aura flows across my chest, down my legs, into my arms, I take a moment to witness and feel its vibration. To appreciate its spiritual essence, its subtle yet powerful beauty. And now I decide to move a certain part of my body, starting with my arm. But before even moving it, I notice how just this *decision* to move my arm has caused a shift in my inner light toward my arm. And now, as I do move my arm, I observe how my entire arm ignites with light, this light being the catalyst energizing the action. I watch in wonder as my body is moved by the energy of the soul.

To again appreciate this phenomenon, I move that arm once more, very slowly this time, and I watch the warm pooling of light that happens in my arm, as well as the force in the light that launches the movement. Shifting my body in this way, under the influence of light, feels so good, so powerful. I turn my attention to another part of my body and again feel light flowing there; I observe as a spark in the light initiates the movement of that part of my body.

By performing actions in this way—by being aware of my inner light and using its energy and flow as the catalyst for the action—I bring purity and power into my movements. In the presence of light, each one of these simple activities—be it rocking from side to side, or walking, or engaging with others—becomes blissful, meaningful, and divine. And as I go forward into the day, carrying a reservoir of light within me, I let the radiance of my soul cascade out into my movements—a beautifully clean, outward flow. My every action is fueled by spirituality and light, and meaning permeates my day.

## Igniting the Furnace Within

The human species ... now *that* is one ingenious phenomenon! As if the wonder of our physical makeup wasn't enough, there's our inner dimension of spirit to marvel at, that experiential inner space that is as wide as the universe yet unseen to the human eye. Kind of mind-boggling, right?

But how aware are we of our very own inner space? How well do we know the paths that crisscross the plains of our spiritual landscape? Most of us, certainly, spend far more time being conscious of the physical world around us than the subtle world inside us. When this happens, we start relying on the outside world for happiness, motivation, and support. And then, if things aren't going our way, our enthusiasm for life can begin to dwindle.

When we do find ourselves feeling a little listless, unmotivated, or blue, we need to reengage our spiritual awareness. By rekindling that pure flame within, we can fill ourselves with its fiery strength and reconstruct our foundation from within.

I look within, and in the darkness and silence of my inner sanctum, I see a spark of light. It is small, and admittedly a little dim, but it's there nonetheless. As always, it is shining, showing me it's still very much alive. I now imagine a cool breeze entering my inner world, and as air wafts in, it oxygenates this inner spark. Immediately, what was just a speck of light a moment ago starts burning with more force.

As the breeze continues to flow in, I sit back and watch and *feel* as my inner light starts coming to life, as it grows bigger and brighter—no longer a spark, but a flame now. And this flame dances. Still the breeze fans in, oxygenating it, nourishing it, encouraging it. Before I know it, the flame has become a fire, and the warmth of this inner burn feels so good, so firmly rooted in my heart, so strong. My fire blazes with a potent spiritual energy that spreads outward, feeding me with its light as heat diffuses through my body, as its golden vigor fills my entire being. I feel a distinct power in the fire, and in the power is bliss.

My body feels this power and absorbs this bliss. This inner light is a bright catalyst, giving me forward momentum, lifting me, giving me my life-glow, my fuel, my creative existence. And when I begin to move my body and interact with others, I feel myself being driven forward by the force in this light. My fire dances within, guiding me, taking me accurately and confidently forward. It beams out its energy through my body, straightening and emboldening my posture. It radiates out through my face, brightening my smile and my eyes. It uplifts my mood, my being, my existence.

I hold on to the warmth and power of my inner fire, letting it fuel my determination, my confidence, my passion. I stride forward, feeling thoroughly alive, my inner world brimming with the intensity and force of spirit. I am unstoppable as I march onward in my journey through life.

## Oxygenating the Soul

*The body is the temple of the soul.* We've all heard this analogy, reminding us of the importance of our body in enabling the soul to express its array of exquisite qualities in the physical world. However, while we seldom forget the presence of our body, we tend to overlook our inner spiritual light. It's then that we need to breathe life back into the soul, reminding us of its presence and beauty.

By emerging the experience of the soul as often as possible and feeling its divine shimmer, we become adept at tapping into its spring of life. At the same time, we restore that much-needed balance to our physical and spiritual existence.

———

I visualize the soul as a star behind my eyes. I remind myself of what spirit feels like by simply allowing the soul and its energy to come to the forefront of my consciousness. In an instant, I feel my very own gentle yet unwavering pulse of original life. I sense its glow as a soft, comforting pressure point inside my head. A calming energy emerges from it, a spreading of its warmth, first across my forehead, then through my face, and now down my entire body.

As the soul's soothing energy trickles through me, a deep feeling of relaxation and renewal falls over me. So clean is this current of light working its way across the

interior of my being, so all-encompassing is the warmth
of its influence, that I sense a flushing of toxins, a removal
of waste as this sparkling river of life swishes through and
scours all in its path. I let the light circulate all around my
body, watching as it rinses and clears my body of impurities.

I now return my focus to its source, to that glow behind
my eyes, and although I can already feel the soul's energy,
I'd like to experience it more vividly, more tangibly. To do
so, I take in a slow, deep breath of air, directing this inward
flow of oxygen to the very location of the soul. Breathing into the light behind my eyes, watching as my breath
comes into contact with the soul, as this oxygen-rich stream
touches spirit, I feel the soul spark to life. Immediately it
begins to burn brighter, becoming more radiant, more
powerful. I breathe in again, this time straight to the center
of the soul, and again I feel its glow enlarging, becoming
purer, more potent. I inhale as many times as I wish, each
time energizing the soul more, enhancing its light further,
firing up its glow more brightly. I feel my head filling with
its radiance as the soul's glow intensifies. My face is glowing
now, bright, golden light shining out from my forehead, my
cheeks, my eyes.

I take a moment to enjoy this glow, to feel its spread of
warmth across my face, down my neck, and through my
entire body until it reaches the tips of my toes. My whole
body beams with light and spiritual vigor, originating from
that small, concentrated spark at the center of my forehead. As the soul continues to oxygenate with each successive in-breath, as its glow becomes brighter and wider, my

body reflects this shimmer. I, the soul, am nourishing and rejuvenating the home of my body with my spiritual light. My body radiates with health as I step out into this day, invigorated by my vibrant shimmer within.

## Reemerging My Power

Located at the center of our being is the soul, a powerhouse of energy that we can draw on whenever we wish. By reconnecting regularly with its essence and tapping into its sacred waters, we allow spirit to touch every aspect of our lives, giving ourselves the most natural boost available.

Without wasting another minute, let's venture off in search of spirit and draw from its prolific pool of life.

———

Deep within me is an energy that keeps me moving, thinking, being. It keeps me alive. To remind myself of this mystical force I carry with me, I look inward with the view of exploring what it really means to be a soul. And so, directing my gaze toward my inner world, I touch the brilliance of the soul.

This spark of life, however, is not something separate from me. It is me. I am this vibrant light. I am the soul. The conscious me exists at the center of this light. And though this light is inside my body, it is distinct from my body. I, the soul, *have* a body, and I can feel that physicality here, surrounding me. And for the next few moments, all I do is quietly observe what it feels like to be inside yet separate from my body. I am made up of spiritual light, and my body is entirely physical. I exist as light, and beyond that light is my body.

I now explore what it feels like to be the observer seated behind these eyes, looking out through them as I witness the physical dimension from my spiritual seat within. The world is busy; I am quiet. I feel secure here inside my body, and although I may be small—just a spark of light—I am infinitely strong and stable. In my existence as light, indeed, I am invincible. It is within this light where my power resides—the power of purity, of peace, of love.

Settled here, at the very center of my own light, I observe my glow. I watch as light streams outward from my epicenter, from this glow of consciousness that is me, and I see how unblemished this light is. It is spiritual light, and thus innately pure. As often as I wish, I can return to this stable space within, to my room of light, to my domain of spirit. This simple inward journey reminds me of all my potential, my peace, my power. It takes me back to the richness of the soul. I need to just look within and open up to my glow of life.

And now, receptive to this very light, I let it flow into my feelings, into my movements, into my interactions. My inner spark keeps my bearings facing forward, keeps me moving toward that very best version of myself. It keeps me on the path toward the real me. As I carry on with this amazing journey of life, I fill my existence with beautiful, inspiring light.

## Probing the Body-Soul Divide

Differentiating between the body and the soul, at least in theory, is easy; the body is physical and mortal, while the soul is nonphysical and immortal. But what does this distinction *feel* like? Can we distinguish between the two *experientially*?

The following exercise in delineating the body-soul divide guides us into precisely this experience.

—

I inhale deeply, and following my breath, I go within. Seated behind my eyes inside this physical instrument of flesh, I take a moment to feel my body as it exists around me. I pay attention to the experience of being surrounded by this visible mass that is my body, of all its weight and substance. But who is the "me" experiencing this? Where am I observing the physicality of it all from? The answer is, of course, my consciousness, my soul. I, this spiritual energy, am seated within my body, yet distinctly separate from my body. I, the soul, am aware of and feel my body's bulk as it surrounds me. From within, I look out through my organs of sight, these eyes. I listen with these ears. I smell with this nose. I taste with this tongue. I feel through this skin. My body is my vehicle to experience life as it exists around me, to express life as it exists in me.

In order to understand more deeply this body-soul divide, I perform an experiment: remaining centered in the seat of the soul here behind my eyes, I tilt my head gently over to the left, then back over to the right. I remind myself that it is I—this point of spiritual, conscious energy within—moving my body. I am this central energy giving instructions. From this vantage point within, I am experiencing physicality—in this case, the weight of my head. I make my head roll left and right again, very slowly, very consciously, all the while aware of myself within, existing as a spark of spiritual light, giving instructions to my body. Seated here in my cockpit behind my eyes, I, the soul, am moving my head. It is also from here—the conscious mind—that I am observing this movement of my head, that I am feeling its weight.

Once again, centered and still within this inner space, I observe my head rolling slowly from side to side. I now bring my head to a standstill, taking a moment to look out through these eyes and examine the world from my inner space. I see my surrounds as they exist outside of me.

Now, shifting my focus back to my entire body as it exists around me, I notice its shape, its form. This simple act of witnessing my body from the detached perspective of the soul brings a distinct calm to my body. I notice how relaxed and settled it is. And yet, although I feel my body, it is clearly distinguishable from me. It belongs to me—but is not me. I am this living energy within, this spark from which my thoughts and feelings emerge. Sadness, happiness, love—they all emerge from the soul. I look straight into myself now, into my very consciousness, into the center of the soul, and it becomes patently clear that I am made up purely of light. Still, sacred light. I exist within this light. Being here in the light, it's like I have returned to the womb. I am surrounded by my very own warm, protective glow, by my very own spiritual life force.

I now observe my shimmer, my energy field emanating from my center-point and radiating outward. Enjoying my very own iridescence, my own vitality, I feel my light begin to grow in intensity and in size. It starts to fill the spaces within my body. As it expands, I choose to send waves of loving, healing energy to my body. I direct the flow of my spiritual energy toward all parts of this incredible physical instrument that carries me about so efficiently day after day, this instrument that enables expression of my spirituality. And I express that spiritual beauty now, in all its fullness, by gently guiding my vibration downward through my body. I feel a bright warmth spreading through my limbs, a flow of healing, clean light. And the light of spirit continues to disperse its warmth, streaming into all the corners of my body. It feels so good, giving energy to my body in this way, feeding it with spiritual light.

Sitting here, I am perfectly aware of my spiritual seat within this body, perfectly aware of how I operate my body from here, of how I am sending the energy of renewal into my body to effect healing. In doing this, I am patently aware of how the body and soul are separate entities, yet exist together in a sacred dance of cooperation. From the center of my being, I continue to uplift my body with healing, spiritual light.

## Playing with Perfection

Is perfection possible? Or is it merely something ascetics strive for, yet possibly never achieve?

While a path toward perfection may seem overly ambitious, what if we were to break it down into smaller, bite-size chunks? What if we set out to achieve perfection—even if only temporarily—of one specific virtue?

*In this moment, I summon stillness. And I see it shimmering up ahead, patiently coaxing me forward. I walk toward it and step into its silent embrace. A hush falls over, and my world turns perfectly still.*

What if every day for just a few minutes—or heck, a few *seconds*—we truly experienced a virtue in its fully realized form? We'd quickly become adept at emerging this quality in our hearts and expressing it in its truest, cleanest form.

*Perfect stillness exists in me. I feel its warmth resonating in my heart, its beauty shining through my being. I let it out now, showering my surrounds with the fragrance of stillness.*

Let's reach for the stars and challenge ourselves to taste perfection. Let's dive into the laboratories of our hearts and minds and investigate what perfect peace, love, or happiness feels like. Let's give ourselves a chance at playing with that elusive diamond called perfection.

I step inward in search of the light. Before I even see it, I feel it: a warm, spiritual glow coming from within. I see it now, too, shining brightly at the center of my being, and I move toward it. Taking another step inward, I enter the beautiful orb within me. I seat myself comfortably inside its warm space and find myself in a world filled with silence, with clarity, with simple beauty. I am seated in a place where perfection really can exist—and perhaps already does. Resting at the center of my own divine light, I realize this is all I am: light. And is light not inherently perfect? Indeed, is it even possible to blemish light? Surely not. And so, here in this bright inner space that vibrates with the echo of perfection, I choose to explore the radiance that surrounds me. I choose to explore my own spiritual light.

In this space within my own brilliance, I can experience firsthand what my energy feels like. I can experience what it is to be me: that pure, eternal spirit. The soul and its qualities are perfect. Nothing exists here *but* perfection. And my perfection reveals itself through my feelings and my expression of them. My realized self is revealed through my perfect peace, my contentment, my love. These qualities shine like jewels within, untainted. And I feel their flawless shine. Here, within my own illuminated inner space, I am surrounded by unadulterated light. By perfection.

In order to explore an individual virtue, I start off by merely feeling my light as a warm glow within. Now, I choose my virtue—peace—and feel peace within my light.

And this simple experience—my light, saturated with peace—brings about a change in me. A deep hush of peace blankets my entire being. I shine with peace. Peace-filled light circulates through me. Peace surrounds me. I emit an aura of peace. This is perfection in action: me, very naturally, exuding peace in its purest form—as light. Seated in my spiritual heart, surrounded by light, I touch, and feel, and play with peace in its perfect state.

I bring perfection to the surface via light, via a feeling in the light, and offer it to the world in its original form. I can offer whichever quality I wish for—love, happiness, purity, or silence—first to myself, then to my surrounds. I can emit perfection through my light. Sitting below the surface in my quiet inner world, I am in touch with my essence, with my original being. And how beautifully I shine, how brightly I shimmer, how rich my heart is with light.

## Becoming a Weightless, Shining Star

When we get out into the countryside and observe the myriad of effervescence hovering in the sky—that wash of stars!—we're sometimes met with feelings of giddy lightness. It can even feel like we're being pulled upward into that panoramic sky above— and before we know it, we too are suspended in midair, weightless and bright, indeed another sparkling star.

Let's invite that feeling of drifting upward so that we too can float among the stars.

⌒

I lie back and watch—or imagine that I am watching—the night sky. What lies above me is a vast plain dotted with a sea of shining stars. Each star appears so unburdened, so weightless as it floats in the air, shimmering unassumingly with its own light.

I wonder what it would be like to be one such star, suspended high above the earth, simply emitting my own natural light. How would it feel to exist in that state of giving, just releasing an endless flow of light and energy into my surrounds? Wishing to experience this feeling, I consciously grant myself the freedom to drift upward to the stars. I simply let go, and up I float, to a place among those shining lights in the sky. Up here, I feel my body disappearing, disappearing—and all of a sudden, it's gone. All that remains of me is pure light—indeed, I am another star in this spread of celestial effervescence. I take note of what it feels like to be suspended in space, to hover in a weightless state like these stars around me. I, too, exist in a world that is open and free.

I become aware of my light as it exists within me, warm and bright. And I now offer this light to the stars around me. As I do so, I feel a stream of purity originating from somewhere deep inside me, flowing outward. This energy feels so natural, so powerful. I realize how unlimited I am in giving. This light, emerging from my center, has no beginning and no end. It simply exists in me, will *always* exist in me. I can use it as I wish to heal myself and to heal my surrounds. And now, from this vantage point up above, I shift my attention toward the earth. I look to the slowly rotating globe of beauty below and send my light home, toward all the souls inhabiting our planet. I shower my light onto all that vibrant life down below. I send them my energy, and I send them love.

As my light continues to emerge and stream outward in a torrent of giving, I feel full. Full with the knowledge that I can bring benefit to all. Full with the belief, and now the experience, that light suffused with love is indeed the answer. I am a sparkling star, and I uplift the world through the energy of my living, loving light.

# Chapter 10
# Unity

Humanity has become fragmented, with "us" and "them" distinctions surfacing in areas like nationality, race, gender, and sexual identity. We have forgotten the fundamental principle that we are one species, all looking for the same things in life: love, peace, and happiness. Yet instead of observing the commonalities that tie us together, we seem more habituated to seeing our differences. As a result, our default setting becomes a heart that is more closed than open and an attitude leaning toward intolerance.

Let's return to human basics and see the similarities that bond us all. Let's open ourselves up and acknowledge that another's wish for a meaningful, peaceful existence is no different from ours. Let's hold on to the ideal that we are spiritual siblings as we pave the way toward becoming the unified, happy human family we all long for.

## Entering the Heart of a Stranger

With around eight billion people living on this planet, it's easy to become indifferent toward strangers. But what if, on occasion, we approached these very strangers from a position of love?

By making the effort, even for the briefest of moments, to look into the hearts and minds of strangers—be it the bank clerk or the passenger beside us on the bus—we give ourselves the chance to acknowledge their inner worlds and all the wisdom they carry within. We see them as someone with a heart full of feelings like ours, enabling us to approach them as we would a friend—with trust and understanding. Before we know it, our experience of them, and their experience of us, will have transformed into something far deeper than a mere transitory interaction.

Children have a natural tendency toward this kind of open-minded, open-hearted mingling; how quickly they connect with other kids, no questions asked! Their innocent curiosity and enthusiasm for life fuels an instant bond with strangers.

Let's become those children once again, curious and enthusiastic—and, above all, nonjudgmental—as we open ourselves up to the inner world of a stranger. We may be pleasantly surprised by what emerges in our hearts—and in theirs!

———

I turn my attention to a stranger in my vicinity. It may be that I'm taking a bus, walking in the street, waiting in line, or dealing with a customer. Whoever is in front of me, I take a second to reflect on who this person really is. I reflect on what is going through their mind in this moment, of all their background stories that may be exerting an influence on their present. I think about the varied journeys they must have taken through life, bringing them to this very place in front of me. My journey, too, has brought me here to them.

Beneath the surface of their mere appearance is a universe of thoughts, feelings, memories, and experiences. I wonder about this inner world of theirs, their set of values, their aspirations, the challenges they may be facing. In many respects, their inner world and their hopes must surely be similar to mine. They, too, must be striving toward a life of peace, love, and happiness. These are the basic pleasures we all strive toward, after all, even if our methods of achieving them differ. The qualities they admire and wish for in their lives are surely no different from mine. They, too, want to progress, to become better versions of themselves, to be more content and wise. Their experience of love may be just like mine. The sadness they feel on seeing a loved one in pain is the same sadness I feel. They are like me in so many ways.

As I reflect on their inner worlds, they cease to be strangers. They become fellow beings. This is my brother, my sister, my kin, on a path so similar to mine. They too are moved by beauty. They too seek meaning. They too hold love in their heart, and sometimes sadness. They too have painful episodes in their past that they are working through.

And now, looking beyond all these emotions and feelings, I peer into their consciousness. I look to their inner light. And I see that light, the spark that moves them forward on their path through life. They are spiritual energy on a spiritual journey, just like me. Their soul radiates with wisdom and with love, as does mine. They are, like me, dynamic, moving, conscious light. Their spirit is beautiful, like mine. We are composed of the same substance, the same inner beauty. We are part of a single spiritual family, and right now, I celebrate this connection. I look into their eyes and give them a warm smile. As I do so, I touch their heart with love. I feel the divine connection we eternally share, and I trust that they, too, feel our spiritual bond.

## Merging of Hearts, Meeting of Minds

The following meditation is especially for the cyclists among us; I simply had to include it, what with cycling and spirituality being such a great match! And not to worry if you're not of the two-wheeler ilk—this meditation can be as effectively applied to walking and running, too.

Cycling (and walking!) is one of the cleanest forms of transport, requiring no external energy source. Spirituality, too, is free of external requirements; all that's needed for a spiritual experience is self-awareness. *I am. I exist. Now.*

Both cycling and spirituality are wonderfully efficient, too. Those who've cycled on flat, windless roads know the speed one can clock up with minimum effort. As for spirituality's efficiency, how fantastic is a brief moment spent in silent communion with spirit, in clearing our mind and elevating our mood, in fueling our life with fresh meaning.

Another feature of cycling is the absence of barriers between us and the environment. We have a full-blown environmental experience from the saddle of our bike, appreciating the sights, the smells, the sounds. We *feel* the sunshine and wind—preferably from behind! Existing in a heightened state of awareness, we begin to see. This enhanced wakefulness—similar to that of a spiritual experience—opens us up to the beauty and radiance of nature. And when we love nature, we begin to find beauty everywhere, as Vincent van Gogh allegedly once said. There's nothing quite like observing a gorgeous sunset over a turquoise ocean from the seat of our bicycle!

So, let's hop on our bikes (or get strolling), as we activate our senses and souls in a vivid, moving meditation.

———

Riding my bicycle (or walking down the road), I become aware of an approaching pedestrian, cyclist, or driver in a car up ahead. I don't necessarily need to make eye contact with them at this point; simply holding their presence in my mind is sufficient. I focus on feeling their energy, their inner light as they approach me. I open myself up to their vibration.

As we come closer and closer to one another, I begin to feel their essence more acutely, that trueness of spirit inside them. I start to sense the spiritual connection we share as our two energies approach one another. And being connected means we can communicate, albeit subconsciously. I can make my spiritual presence known to them. And I do so, sending a wave of goodness, of warmth their way. Now, within the warmth I am offering, I choose to embed a beautiful virtue, with that virtue being the one that naturally emerges in my heart, right now. It may be peace, or love, or stability I feel blossoming inside. I simply let this quality rise in me and stream outward toward them.

I observe how effortlessly my energy pours out and flows their way. I observe as that energy enters them, as my consciousness connects with their consciousness, as my heart merges with theirs. By sending out my vibrant energy, I am touching them with the deepest part of my being. As my light meets their inner world of light, I feel us connecting, becoming entwined, merging into one. I hold on to this spiritual bond as we continue our paths toward each other. I grow this connection, feeling it becoming stronger and brighter as we close in on one another. And finally, as we pass each other, I acknowledge their beauty by establishing eye contact and giving them a warm smile and a nod of the head. They may even acknowledge me, too. And our moment together, that brief sharing of spirituality, is special. We are brothers and sisters, walking similar paths toward oneness and truth.

## Opening My Heart to Love

As inherently social beings, our constant interplay with those around us results in us being affected by others' energy while affecting them with our energy, too. What's more, this sphere of influence we thus have, via the energy we emit, has a far wider impact than we sometimes realize.

Simplistically, we could break the energy we transmit into three kinds: positive, neutral, and negative. We needn't delve into the neutral and negative kinds—we're optimists, after all!—but among the positive energies we give off, love is arguably the one that reigns supreme.

When we focus on and experiment with the energy of love (for example, by projecting it onto passersby), benefit happens in two ways. First, somewhat ironically, *we* draw the initial benefit, with love emerging in our heart and warming us from the inside before it even starts its outward flow. The second benefit belongs, of course, to the recipient; they will, even if only subconsciously, be touched by our love.

Engaging in this kind of subtle world service opens up our heart, steering us automatically onto a path of growth. We experience spirituality in a very practical, intimate way as we bring our inner light to the surface and actively put it to use. Offering the vibration of love—or peace, strength, or silence—is rewarding and educational, not to mention fun!

So, how many strangers crossed my path today? Dozens? Hundreds? Yes, that's how many opportunities we have to share our pure energy and bring our heart—and hopefully theirs, too—into play. This is experiential spirituality—spirituality of the living, breathing variety. This is the growing and connecting of hearts. These may be strangers, but they are also fellow spiritual beings; deep down, their needs are no different from ours. They, too, respond to the magic of love.

If you're wondering where you might practice this projection of energy, try any public place. Even now, in the comfort of wherever you find yourself, imagine you're standing on the platform of a train station. Your train enters the platform, and you glance into one of the coaches, becoming aware of its passengers and their inner worlds. You see them, you feel them—and now, you gently nudge your loving energy out and onto them. Not complicated, right? Just feeling their presence, opening your heart up wide, and sending love right their way. This is spirituality 101—simple, practical, and available to all.

Once we do it, we realize how easy and natural this kind of spiritual service is. And as the warmth flows out from us and onto them, our eyes will soften and our hearts will swell with love's upwelling. Our day will instantly become that much more rewarding and complete.

Let's practice a little love today by entering a heart-to-heart connection with someone in our surrounds. Together, let's build that platform of love.

———

I go quietly within, into the depths of my heart, where all is peaceful and warm. And as I rest here, I begin to feel the seed of a bright, vital energy emerging. It is the energy of love. I take several moments to acknowledge and enjoy this feeling as it gently rises in my heart. I let myself simply relax into this inner expansion of love. I let love exist within, let it vibrate, let it flow like water through me. Just letting it be, letting it grow, letting it influence my present.

And now, from this snug inner space all warmed up with love, I look outward and become aware of the people in my surrounds. I see my fellow beings, each one busy with their own life. I wish to touch them with spirit. To do so, I allow my free-flowing river of love to seep outward, and I direct this pure energy their way. I nudge my clean light toward these beings whose hearts are as warm as mine. I give to them, and this giving feels so natural, so easy. Love's radiance rolls out from me, onto them and into them. As I gaze out, I can feel my eyes soften with the energy of giving, with this simple act of shifting the world toward love. I let love exist in me, let it fill my being and flow freely out into my surrounds. I let it drift toward others and seep into their inner worlds.

This love is real. I know this because I can feel its rich substance, its transformative force as it rises in me and warms the entirety of my being. I can feel the purity of its energy sprouting in me and streaming out from me, connecting me to those in my surrounds. I coexist with all that exist on this planet, each one of us united in the tapestry of love.

## Exploring the Energy of Others

We are all energy, and energy flows—into us, within us, and out of us. By becoming quiet as we look inward, by inviting an open heart and an alert mind, we can get in touch with and experience this energy. We can use it in healing, too: first, on ourselves, as we send it to those areas of our body and mind in need of restoration; and second, on others, as we send it outward.

The simple act of glancing inward with the intention of touching our deepest energy also has the benefit of bringing us smartly into the present. Simultaneously, through the process of experiencing our own subtle energy, we deepen our connection with ourselves, thus enhancing our understanding of who we are. And when we become accustomed to sensing our own spiritual energy, picking up on the energy of others becomes second nature.

Let's experiment with our own and others' energy and, while doing so, learn some deep truths about humanity that no book could ever teach us.

———

I sit quietly, closing my eyes if I wish, and I become aware of what it feels like to be alive. What is this energy that exists within, revealing life? Indeed, what is life? What is at the heart of this experience of being alive? I wait patiently for this energy, showing me I am alive, to surface and reveal its spark.

Ah, there it is—that small inner vibration of life. Taking a moment to enjoy this flicker of vitality within, I acknowledge that this is uniquely my energy. This is the me, existing at the center of my being. I feel a deep tenderness, observing my energy in this way. Yes, this really is me. Nobody but me emits this exact pulse, this precise spark of life. How beautiful I am!

I now shift my focus to beyond me, to someone in my immediate surrounds. I sense a distinct energy coming from them, too—their own glowing life force. They, too, silently and naturally emit a beautiful energy. Their radiance is gentle and soothing and, like mine, unique in its vibration. Just sitting here, feeling the energy they emit, is a meditation in itself.

I go deeper into enjoying their tremor of life, into experiencing their brilliant light. Their energy is coming my way, encircling me now. I touch its purity, feel its spiritual warmth. Whether they know it or not, they are giving off an aura that is open and inviting, an energy coming from that deep space of goodness inside them. I know this because I can feel that goodness. Their energy is filled with their peace, their love, their compassion. This person is my spiritual friend. We are united by the same deep vision of a global shift toward mutual respect, toward love, toward spiritual unity. We all desire deep connections with one another. And here, beside them, with them, experiencing their essence, I celebrate our togetherness of spirit and our purity of vision. We belong to one large, loving family, linked through our subtle yet influential thread of spirit.

## Embracing the Unity of Spirit

The social world we live in presents us with opportunities aplenty to connect with other beings. Physically, we do so through words, body language, or touch. Spiritually, we're able to consciously direct our inner energy—our *spiritual* energy—outward, sharing our warmth in subtle, unseen ways.

We can feel others' energy, too, by intentionally becoming aware of their inner worlds. This "spirit-sensing" is a subtle yet powerful exercise that guides us toward social oneness.

Let's embrace our sense of community by experimenting with the unifying nature of spirit.

I focus my attention on a person in my surrounds—perhaps not even looking directly at them, but being aware of their presence, of their existence, of the energy they are giving off right now. I follow that energy to their inner world, into their mind, all the way to its source. It's as though I've floated into their body—into their consciousness—with my consciousness. I am in that quiet, creative space behind their eyes.

Seated in their inner world, I can see and feel the silent room that exists here. I can explore their inner expanse. It is very still—and yes, so similar to the silent room of my own mind. I, like this person, am someone who reveres peace and stillness. They, like me, possess a world filled with delicate beauty within. They too appreciate refined feelings, like harmony and calm. Like me, they have an extraordinary mind capable of incredible creativity. Their mind, like mine, sparkles like a ripple-free lake. They too are filled with an array of remarkable memories and experiences. We share so much. And in this moment of togetherness, I can appreciate the similarity between their inner world and mine. Here are two worlds, separated by matter, yet so alike. In this coming-together of spirit, I clearly understand how we are all one human family, divinely connected. We belong together as one human species, inhabiting one planet. Sharing love among ourselves should be so natural, so easy—and can be, when we empathize with others by reaching out with our hearts and minds and considering their inner worlds.

Right now, I send this person in front of me pure feelings and positivity. I send the warm contents of my heart toward their heart. I send them my energy, my love. And in this moment of spiritual connection, this person may well sense my presence. They too may have a spontaneous realization that love is natural and easy, and an essential part of our everyday life.

# Chapter 11
# The Universal Spirit

The names we have given God are wide and varied—Jehovah, Shiva, Jah, the Almighty. The one name we are all familiar with, though, is *God*. Yet for some, "God" feels too authoritarian, and instead they opt for softer names, like Divine Mother or Universal Spirit. Others may even choose to alter God's name according to the experience they're after. When looking for a gentler experience involving peace, love, or healing, a more feminine name might feel appropriate. For a boost of strength, focus, or courage, they may choose something more masculine—or, indeed, "God."

As mentioned in the introduction, I've chosen to simply use the name *God* for the sake of consistency. At the same time, I refer to God via the feminine pronoun, *she*, to emphasize the healing and love our world is so thirsty for. But feel free to substitute *God* with whatever name you feel most comfortable with. The more personal we can make our meditations, after all, the more deeply we can connect to divinity.

Regardless of the name we settle on for God, her essence remains the same. She is both gentle and powerful—and, above all, loving. We can touch that love, too, by inviting her sublime influence into our lives and filling ourselves with the vibration of spirit.

Let's open ourselves up to an experience of divinity, now.

## Moments in the Presence of God

Throughout the ages, God has been the subject of endless reflection and debate as humans endeavor to understand what this higher power is all about. Who is this being we call God? And what would it feel like to be seated in front of a power so ethereal, so universal?

By quieting our minds, focusing our thoughts, and opening our hearts to the infinite world of spirit, we can listen to and tune in to God's vibration. By placing our consciousness squarely before her multifaceted, boundless light, we can find out for ourselves what this great being is all about.

Let's have that meeting with God, right now.

―――――

I settle my body through a series of deep, conscious breaths. My limbs, my torso, and my eyes are all comfortable and relaxed. My mind, too, feels at peace, and with the peace comes clarity. I feel a clean, calm space opening up within, a place granting me the freedom to explore as far and wide as I wish.

I now imagine myself traveling upward into the spiritual realm, into that silent realm of light. I am simply taking myself there with my consciousness, freeing the soul through the power of my mind. And in an instant, I am above all the clutter and noise of our world and in the dimension of spirit. I am in the original home of peace and purity. I take a moment to listen to that peace, to feel that purity. And in this opening up of my senses, I detect some great energy filling my surrounds, a distinctly divine vibration filtering through the vastness of this spiritual plane. Indeed, I sense the presence of God.

I look into the distance, across this open landscape, and see the most inviting, golden light. And yes, I recognize this light; it is God I see glowing in front of me. I feel myself being drawn closer, being pulled forward by my instinctual attraction to this gentle light. And as I approach God, I begin to feel the warmth in her light—a full, welcoming warmth. I am indeed in the company of divinity. Now, as I enter God's field of light, a stillness fills me. I feel the deep hush of my surrounds seeping into me, blanketing me in silence. In this silence of being, my focus is rigged on God's light alone. She fills my entire vision now, and within her light, I sense a soothing, open space, inviting me deeper in. There is profound wisdom here; I feel it, and I can tap into it, right now. I just need to be quiet and listen to the light, to the sacred presence within the light. And as I look into the light, into the silence within the light, I discover true tranquility. This is the very home of peace.

While admiring this wonderworld of silence and calm, I feel God's light entering me. I open my heart to this inward flow, absorbing every ounce of her love, her wisdom, her fullness. Seated in front of God, it all becomes so easy. All that's needed is me casting my gaze into her pristine depths, into her otherworldly beauty—and instantly she takes me up in her warm embrace. And now I look even deeper into the light, so deep that before I know it, I am right inside God's light. Her loving vibration surrounds me, touching me with her purity, with her silence.

I can now see for myself who this incredible being is. I can experience all that exists within her light. I can touch and understand God's inner world, God's personality, God's heart. And as I observe the reality of God from inside her light, as I experience her infinite depths, her beauty continues to flow into me. Being here, I am taking on God's immaculate nature. In the presence of God, I am very naturally being filled by her light, absorbing her vibration, feeling her essence entering me. Seated here, infused with divine light, I am a reflection of God's beauty. I radiate her light, and my world is rich and complete. I am touching God, God is touching me, and we exist together in a powerful merging of light.

## The Light at the End of the Tunnel

We've all heard the accounts by survivors of near-death experiences where they describe themselves having been irresistibly drawn toward a warm, loving light. Inevitably, this encounter with divinity changes them profoundly; they come out of the experience with a fresh, inspired attitude toward life and a renewed appreciation for spirituality.

With a little silence and focus—and no brushes with death!—
we too can take ourselves into that experience. We too can meet
the highest light.

———

I relax my body, letting it settle and become warm, letting
it feel good. My body is calm now, my heart still. I visualize darkness ... cool, quiet, peaceful darkness. And into
the darkness I go, appreciating its emptiness, its silence. I
rest here for a few moments, just taking the silence into
me, absorbing its tranquility. And now, glancing up, I see
a speck of light ahead, far off in the distance. I realize that
I am in a tunnel, and that little light, up ahead, is beckoning me. I recognize some deep purity in it, something very
sacred, and I see that I am being pulled, very gently, toward
its glow.

As I drift forward, approaching the light and watching
as it gets bigger and brighter, I start to feel a warm presence
within the light. My entire focus is on the light now, my
curiosity drawing me in, urging me closer so that I might
learn more about this fascinating energy in front of me. As
I look into its essence, it becomes patently clear that this is
no ordinary light. Its radiance is unique and, most notice-
ably, alive. There is a distinct energy, a personality, within
this light, and that personality is beckoning me. This light
wants to be with me, wants to comfort me. I continue to
move closer to its brilliance, and as I do so, I become more
and more aware of the life within the light.

Looking deeply into the light now, I feel myself falling into serenity. This light is lulling me into calmness, into comfort. I continue to go closer, pulled gently by the mystical forces within the light. It's like I am simply meant to be with the light. Already I sense and know we are destined to be together. And that's all I want right now: to go deeper and deeper, to be pulled further and further into the beauty and the warmth, into the tranquility of this light.

To allow this to happen, I relax fully, releasing every part of my being, and I let this force in front of me take over. I surrender to my attraction, to my curiosity, to my wish to be united with this light, and I allow myself to drift straight into its depths. Within the orb of calm before me lies healing; this much I know. I can feel the full potential of this light to bring wholeness to my being. This light isn't mere light. It is divine radiance. I am being pulled toward the highest spirit, toward the very being we have struggled to understand throughout the ages. I am moving toward original love, toward original life. I am approaching a being who has forever existed in a perfect state, a being replete with purity, a being we have named God.

I flow forward, into her warmth, into her embrace, into her heart. I am deep within God's glow now, and her vibrational light surrounds me. Her radiance flows into me and fills me. I am one with her energy, and I feel this energy inside me. Her light is rolling through me, light suffused with healing power. I am being restored by God's light. I am being transformed by the love within the light. *Ah*, so this is what perfect love feels like. How pure it is! I am in the light, and the light surrounds me. As it enters my being from all directions and circulates through me, it enriches me, heals me, uplifts me. I am at one with the highest, most loving, sentient light. I am with God, and, this moment, perfect.

## Infusing Life with Spirit

I am sure that we, as meditators, would largely go along with the premise that we are spiritual beings enjoying a physical experience, rather than physical beings enjoying the occasional spiritual experience. As spiritual beings, then, should our lives not be permeated with peace and love? Spirit is, after all, inherently enlightened, is it not?

Unfortunately, the physical world has a tendency of "getting in the way," shifting our focus away from our spiritual nature and onto the complexities of a material existence. We get caught up in living life, and before we know it, we've all but abandoned our spiritual spark.

So how, then, can we sustain spiritual consciousness in the inherent physicality of our day-to-day existence? Maybe what's needed is a paradigm shift; what if, instead of struggling to *remind* ourselves to be spiritual, we struggled to *forget* our spiritual side? What if our inner light was such a constant feature in our lives, so deeply embedded in our hearts, that to forget our spiritual nature was all but impossible? Every waking moment would be experienced as something elevated and meaningful, and to live without that profundity and wisdom would be unthinkable. Feeling a divine presence would be the norm, and our path through life would be shrouded, very naturally, in light. Living under the canopy of God's warm presence while going about the bustle of our day would be second nature. In touch with her subtle radiance, our every movement would be empowered by light.

Sound far-fetched? Perhaps—but the truth is, good habits are surprisingly easy to create. By setting regular reminders to connect, however briefly, with our inner light and the light of God, we can instill empowering habits of bringing spirituality into our lives. Every hour, I remind myself to touch my light; every second hour, I touch God's. These few minutes invested daily in spirituality will bring a sense of depth and meaning into what might otherwise have been just another ordinary day. By routinely reigniting our subtle spiritual connections, we can make operating in the presence of light something natural—and easy, too. Radiance should surely, after all, be a constant feature of every spiritual being's existence!

Let's take that small step toward making our life one beautiful meditation as we infuse our worlds with light.

———

I visualize God's light. I see its beauty, its softness, its warmth. I imagine it to be a normal part of my world, always there, just like the sun. It's therefore entirely natural that, in this moment, I feel God's clean light shining down on me. Knowing how beneficial this light is to my well-being, I allow myself to become that sponge, soaking up God's golden shimmer, taking in her substance, letting her warm me, nourish me, renew me. Right now, I am absorbing the essence of God's energy deeply into me, so deep that it becomes part of me, a constituent of my being.

I happily concede that God is a constant presence in my life, simply there, always. She is like the sun: bright and warm, powerful and giving. I move and live with this companionship of the universal spirit. She is constant in her comfort, constant in her light—and I feel that constancy as she fills me with divinity, right now. I sense how, in this moment, she is giving me the strength and power to be who I want to be. She is inviting me to be the highest me. Even as I go about my daily activities, as I engage in conversations with others, her light is like a stream of inspiration from above, saturating me, encouraging me, energizing me. She illuminates my body, warms my heart, brightens my mind. There is simply no reason to move out of the spiritual sunlight. It uplifts me and brings meaning to my most basic actions. It can bring bliss into my movements, too. And I experiment with this potential for bliss.

Before I move my arm, I feel God's light entering me, flowing into my arm, warming it with her presence. And now, as I move my arm very slowly, I feel God's light energizing this movement, streaming through all the corridors of my arm. This basic action, done in her presence and with her light, fills me with bliss. This simple shifting of my body in the company of divine light feels so good, so powerful.

I turn my attention to another part of my body, again feeling the glow of God's light illuminating that area before I move it. Again, I feel a flow of bliss as the area is lit up with Gods' spiritual vibration, as her light swirls inside my moving body, producing a current of delicious warmth. My movements are smooth, sublime, inspired by light.

And now, as I continue my day, as I maneuver through life, I take God's companionship with me. I hold on to her light. I am in touch with the spiritual sun. All that's needed is a simple reminder to myself that she is there. Divine sunlight shines, and shines constantly. She releases her energy onto me—always giving, always nurturing. My heart is open to God's vibration, meaning nothing can stop this inward stream of exquisite light. It fills every aspect of my world, floods every corner of my being, igniting both body and mind. I walk forward in the presence of sacred, empowering light.

This subtle connection I feel, this personal line I have straight to God cannot be broken. We are tied together by the bond of spirituality. We are parent and child, our conscious minds eternally linked. Walking hand in hand with the beautiful light, this moment is rich and meaningful, and my existence is full.

## Colored by God's Company, Touched by Her Light

Our thoughts can be like errant children, lacking focus as they dart off in every direction imaginable. We'd do well to rein them in on occasion, especially those pesky negative ones. But controlling our thoughts, unfortunately, is far from easy, unless…

Unless we are in the presence of God.

Seated before the deep, transcendent light of God, is it even *possible* to have negative or trivial thoughts? By placing our consciousness in front of God's and giving ourselves the space and time to be touched by her power, we emerge thoughts of the most enriching, optimistic kind. And beautiful thoughts lead to beautiful feelings, especially when touched by the spark of the divine.

So, how do we go about initiating that meeting with God? One way is through reflecting on who God is, and a useful way to launch this reflection is to first manifest God in front of us. We can do this by visualizing God simply as light. Once we feel the warmth and shimmer of that light, we dive deeper in by having a conversation with the light. Remember, this isn't simply light we're talking to. It's sacred, sentient light. It's *God's* light. And by asking questions and reflecting on spirituality in the presence of the radiance that is God, we can begin accessing all that lies within the light. We can experience God's personality firsthand in its true, unadulterated state.

Let's open our hearts and minds and move toward God. Let's discover for ourselves the impact her light—and the personality within that light—can have on our thoughts and feelings, and indeed our lives.

My thoughts are easily influenced by my surrounds. And while that influence is sometimes bright and inspiring, it can steer me in the wrong direction, too. What I am looking for now is that bright, inspiring influence. And for this, I look upward to the brightest, most uplifting being. I look toward the light of God. And there she is, right before me, her soft radiance shimmering like the sun.

As I lean into her light and touch its shimmer, I am immediately reminded of the eternal connection that exists between us. Her loving light binds us to one another, and right now, in this moment of togetherness, we celebrate our unlimited connection. Moving closer to her light, toward her welcoming embrace, I feel her inviting me further in. It's as though she wants me to be with her so that I can draw on her power, making my life fuller and deeper. And I let it happen. I allow myself to drift into her glowing warmth. Here, surrounded by God's silent, accepting light, I feel the influence of this sacred presence on my mood. I observe the quality of my thoughts and feelings and notice how they automatically reflect God's beauty, how they resemble the purity emerging from God's heart. My thoughts and feelings glow as they echo God's essence, as they are touched by this pristine energy I am seated within. I am being filled with the highest light.

Resting here, connected to God, I exist in a state of inspired positivity. And even as I return to the consciousness of my physical reality, I stay in touch with God's light. I hold on to the thread connecting my world with hers and walk forward with energy and enthusiasm. I move within the glow of God's uplifting light.

## Walking toward the Light

Ancient tales are filled with the miracles of guardian angels, protecting pilgrims as they soldier forward on their journey toward self-realization. But do these angelic beings really exist, or are they simply fanciful thinking, created to make us feel spiritual and secure?

Be they fact or fiction, the role we've ascribed to these subtle beings is somewhat interesting: ethereal safeguards, hovering over us as we navigate our way through life. They have a guiding function, too, nudging us constantly toward a life of meaning and positivity—implying that every step we take in the company of our guardian angel is one that brings us closer to our highest self. By staying in the awareness of their benevolent light, we are automatically pulled toward where we need to be.

Although it may all sound too good to be true, perhaps the concept of a personal guiding angel *isn't* as far-fetched as we think. After all, isn't that what God does—inspire us to become our highest self as she guides and nurtures us with her subtle, intelligent light?

What's needed, of course, is the *reminder* to see and feel God's loving, empowering light—indeed, her angelic presence. She is right beside us, after all, constantly. It's just that we forget she's there.

Let's remind ourselves right now to connect to God's universal energy as we reunite with our highest, wisest angel. Let's invite her guidance into our lives as we walk our unique path toward contentment and truth.

———

As I take a walk, I imagine a light hovering over my head. It is an all-knowing, all-powerful, comforting light. It is the light of God, that all-encompassing luminescence of the one who cares for me, who guides me constantly. I need to simply open myself up to that guidance, and it will be there. Always. And I feel this light right now. It is strong and bright, and I can't help but smile as I walk forward, feeling the warmth of its presence.

Right now, I choose to go deeper into this relationship with divinity. And the mere decision to nudge my consciousness toward God intensifies her light, allowing me to experience her energy more vividly, more directly. As I am drawn further into her light, I touch more of it, feel it more brilliantly. Walking forward, holding her light in front of me, I tune my vision solely in to her light. Her magnetic attraction pulls me forward, and my every step is a step closer toward the light. My gait feels so smooth, so easy, just flowing toward the light. Her light energizes my movements, and every step becomes an expression of beauty, of radiance.

As I walk, I feel her guiding light pulling me gently toward my purpose—even if it's a purpose I am unaware of. I trust the light implicitly. I instinctively know that this being is taking me on a path toward enlightenment. I feel God's soft enticements signaling me in the right direction, in the direction that will take me toward my highest self. Every step I take is with the light, toward the light, into the light. In the presence of this guardian angel of the universe, every action takes on meaning and depth. My life takes on a new glow as I am coaxed forward by God's light, as I absorb her light and express it with every movement I make, with every step I take. My body shimmers with natural beauty. My mind glows with positivity.

Here, in the presence of divinity, my life feels perfect, and there's nothing more I want. Every movement, every moment, is harmonious and beautiful. God is providing me with what I need. She is my guiding angel, after all. I need to simply place my trust in her, to keep her light in front of me, and I will experience truth and fulfillment in every step. Continuing my path forward, surrounded by the glow of divine light, my movements are graceful and fluid, and my mind is free.

## Celebrating the Godly Connection

Our world is sustained on many levels by the energy of light. Without sunlight and its role in photosynthesis, we'd quickly cease to exist. There's also that more subtle and often overlooked variety of light: spiritual light—unquestionably as critical to our survival!

When we think of the sparkle of the soul, or that of God, we typically visualize bright energy that burns eternally, sustaining life in an unseen yet powerful way. But this spiritual energy is more than mere light; it's light with personality. It's light with untold depth, light that houses original virtue. It's the resting place of purity, peace, and love in their perfect form. By accessing the light—be it ours or God's—we access these qualities in their pristine form and bring them into full life.

What's more, as we bring spiritual light to the surface, negativity simply ceases to exist. In the presence of an energy so clean and powerful, all forms of waste very naturally get pushed aside—and with some genuine focus, even incinerated. Indeed, it's only when we *forget* about spiritual light that we begin to get trapped in negativity's web.

By going within and recognizing our inner light, then going up and placing ourselves before God's light, we quickly realize how similar these two spiritual energies are. Indeed, many believe they are simply part of the same great light. It certainly makes sense that the light of our soul, if not the same light as God's, would at least be composed of a similar substance. After all, as a child of the supreme light, our form and qualities must be related to one another. That's no doubt why, when we contemplate God's beauty, we are given an instant reminder of our own inherent beauty.

Let's take that moment now, appreciating first our light, then God's, before reveling in this unique connection we have with the divine.

———

Sitting peacefully, I look within to my own spiritual light. Maybe it surfaces as a bright, shining star behind my eyes, or as a clean, pure glow inside my heart. I examine this inner light in whatever form and location it reveals itself, simply appreciating the beauty of its sparkle. By finding and listening to my light in this way, I am getting to understand myself better. I am connecting with all that is happening inside me.

Observing my light, I notice the uplifting effect this simple activity is having on my entire being. This, I realize, is all it takes to be uplifted: being mindful of my inner light. So simple an act, yet so profound is its effect. It's a wonder I don't do it more often! All it takes is a cursory glance within to find and touch my light. And by being in the presence of my original light—by feeling the inherently uplifting nature of spirit—a boost is guaranteed.

Now, in that very presence of my inner light, I look upward to the universal light. I gaze in the direction of God and see that she, too, is composed of that same beautiful sparkle. My soul and the soul of God are made up of the same substance: pure, spiritual light. We both give off warmth. And right now, I choose to focus on that warmth; first, mine, as it spreads out from within, bringing comfort to my entire being, to all the spaces inside me. And now, God's warmth, as it streams down onto me, as it encases me in stillness and comfort. I notice that we both emit peace, too. I feel my peace embedded in my light, as well as God's peace in her light. We both radiate the same positive vibration, the same determined light. Our spiritual energy is strong and constant. It empowers. I am empowered by my own light. I am empowered by God's light. I can use light to lift me—and I do that, right now. I feel the glow of my own light energizing my inner world, bringing clarity. I feel the energizing glow of God's light as she draws me toward her illuminated world and fills me with the substance of spirit.

Now, focusing on my own inner light, feeling its warm vibration within, I direct its radiance upward. I bring my light into direct contact with God's light. Our two bright lights merge into one. I am in God's light, and God's light is in me. We are connected, the universal spirit and I, sharing our immaculate energy with each other. I am a child of the highest light, composed of the same pure substance as God: beautiful, virtue-infused light. Our bond is eternal.

## Conversing with God

God is often represented as light; however, if that's all God was—simple light—a relationship with her wouldn't amount to much.

Of course, it's within the *depths* of God's light where her beauty and mystery lie. There, we can touch and experience the bounty of God's qualities.

One of the simplest, most common ways of initiating and sustaining our relationship with God is by conversing with her. When we talk and listen to her—with feeling, from the heart—we get a firsthand glimpse of all she has to offer and why she has been the focus of so much attention and study over the ages.

We're talking about prayer, right? Well, maybe not. Prayer tends to be one-sided in nature—me, talking to God—while a conversation is, by definition, two-way communication. A divine conversation involves us sending our thoughts and energy upward, then pausing to listen for the response.

Let's begin that dialogue with God, now.

———

I place myself before God. Her beautiful orb of light fills my vision, and I feel a great presence within this light. Ah, to be in the company of God...this is the experience mystics have forever been trying to describe. But what exactly is this experience? Who is this being called God, and how do I feel in her presence?

Right now, seated as I am in front of God, spending time with the very being I wish to understand, I have the perfect opportunity to find answers to these questions. And so, to learn firsthand what exists at the heart of this magnificent light I am gazing into, I set off on a journey to find the mysteries embedded at the center of God's light, to discover what God is composed of, to feel the beauty within her light. It's through my direct experience with this sublime light that I can find the answers. To do so, I begin by initiating a conversation with God, by speaking directly to the light.

"I wish to explore your silence, God." I send my thoughts toward the center of this celestial being who shines so beautifully before me. "I wish to touch that deep stillness within your light."

Having sent my message into the light, I edge toward the light, toward the stillness in the light. I move into the serene space of God's heart at the center of the light and rest there, just listening. I listen to the silence echoing within this great chamber of light that surrounds me, appreciating the innate tranquility of being in the presence of God. Ah, so this is what God's mind feels like. This is the abundance one can experience in a world of hallowed silence. And to know more, I go deeper in, deeper into the stillness, deeper into the light.

"I am surrounded by your stillness and your light," I say, keeping my focus squarely on God. "And you draw me in deeper, deeper into your spiritual embrace. I feel your silence. It welcomes me and fills me."

Again, I simply listen to the stillness, letting it welcome me, letting it fill me, letting it guide me into an understanding of the depths of God. As I listen to that silence, I feel God's presence, rich and full, filling the space around me. God is alive, an energy like no other. This is an energy from another world, yet one that I can touch, and absorb, and be with. This is an energy I can communicate with. Here, within the purity of God's energy field, all I need to do is trust the moment as I let go, let my heart guide me to God. All I need do is open myself up to the light and let spirituality happen. And I feel it happening, right now. I feel myself being drawn into God's soft world of light. Again, I speak to her loving presence:

"My heart is open and receptive. I see your energy, and I wish to experience all it has to offer. I wish to understand you more fully. And so, to enhance my relationship with you, I invite your flow into me. I accept your love and your light, letting them stream into me and lift me."

By simply remaining still and focused on God, I give myself over to the experience. I allow God's subtle energy to enter my subtle being. I feel its inward flow, all of God's beauty, all of God's love. My heart embraces the radiance and the might, the fullness of the light, as I let go into spirituality. I release myself into this direct experience of God, and, giving myself entirely over, I swim in her river of light. I am with God; her light and presence are inside me, her magnificence lifts me. I am bathing in the beauty of divinity, my heart wide open, absorbing every beam of God's silence, of God's wisdom, of God's love. I am being nourished and strengthened by the highest light.

## Inhaling Light

Light holds within it an undeniable nurturing force; the sun is a prime example of this, with its inherent capacity in helping initiate and sustain life. Humans, too, are energized by the sun. How we love lapping up those sunbeams on a perfect spring day!

Spiritual light is, in many ways, akin to sunlight, with all its innate power and energy-giving potential. We too can bathe under its canopy, drawing its subtle energy into us, both nourishing and transforming ourselves in the most natural way.

Let's seat ourselves directly in those beams of spiritual light, giving ourselves a reminder of that feel-good factor so inherent in light.

———

I sit quietly and focus on my breathing. As I inhale, I draw air deep into my body; as I exhale, I slowly push it out. With each in-breath, I invite more comfort in; with each out-breath, I relax more. Breathing in, releasing out. And deeper I go, deeper into comfort, deeper into calm.

I now direct my focus upward, toward the light that shines eternally. And there God is, in all her transcendent beauty. I notice her rays of light are directed my way, and I feel them as they come into contact with my skin. An exquisite warmth spreads its way across my body, relaxing me even more. Seated here, gazing into the brilliance of God, I focus on the sensation of God's energy making contact with my skin and dispersing its warmth across me. All I need to do is rest here—aware that I am in the presence of God—to be perfectly content.

I feel a gentle smile lighting up my face, and that smile seeps into my eyes as deep satisfaction sprouts within. This feeling of receiving and absorbing God's pure energy is so rich, so real, so transformative. There is magic in this light—I can feel that magic on my skin, across my body, in my being. With God's flawless light in front of me and her rays of enriching energy flowing onto me, I return to my breathing. But I am no longer breathing in air. I am breathing in light—God's light. I inhale, and I take God's perfect light into my body, watching as it unfurls within, feeling it touch all the crooks and bends of my body with its magic.

Now, as I breathe out, I let my body sink further into peace. Again, I breathe in, taking divine light into the deepest parts of my body. I feel God's glow melting into me, each of my individual cells absorbing its radiance, being energized by its light. And as I continue breathing in light and offering its essence to my receptive cells, I feel myself becoming new. As the light penetrates the furthest reaches of my body, I feel restoration happening within. I am being transformed by the light.

Again, I take in another full breath of light, and I carefully observe the effect it has on me, watching as the light merges with and becomes part of my biological makeup. I feel how it empowers me, purifies me. I observe a miraculous shift happening in me, right before my eyes. I am being moved toward fullness, toward the perfection inherent in light. This time, as I breathe out, I release this light, slowly and purposefully, into the world. I offer this radiance outward.

Again, I inhale God's light, then exhale, giving light to the world. With each in-breath, healing happens in me. With each out-breath, I fill my surrounds with spiritual light, enabling the light to work its magic in healing the world. Inhaling and exhaling God's nourishing light, I am part of a cycle of natural divinity, of self-healing and planetary healing. My connection with God brings about visible growth in me, and I share that growth—that return to fullness—with my surrounds.

## Listening to Love

God can fulfill many roles—mother, father, counselor, guide, healer, and friend—with each role unlocking different virtues and traits of God. Depending on the experience we're looking for in our meditations, we can choose the role we'd like her to fulfill. If we're in search of love, reflections on God as our mother may be apt. If it's wisdom we're after, we may choose to converse with the guide or the counselor in God. For warmth, we could connect with God as our dearest friend.

Catching the essence of God's subtle messages offered via these different roles needn't be a complicated, overly religious rigmarole, either. All that's needed is us taking moments out of our day, becoming still and listening for that divine whisper of advice directed solely our way.

Sitting quietly, I look in God's direction. And I see her, in her form of light. And within that light lies a universe. By entering that universe, I can touch all God's layers, all her roles. I can be with my loving spiritual parent, my profoundly wise guide, my heartfelt healer, my dearest friend.

I take some time to just observe this light, to appreciate the refined beauty shimmering so gently in front of me. And as I look into the light, I see its rays are directed my

way. Keeping my gaze firmly on the light, I start to listen.
And as I am listening, I find myself being drawn into the
light. What message does God have for me? She knows what
I need, after all, and by tuning in to her message, I can be
guided, subtly and lovingly, in the right direction. I just need
to concentrate on and listen to the light, to her beauty, to
her stillness. She will offer me a soft experience, an experience imbued with wisdom, an experience coming from that
all-knowing realm of spirit. For me to catch her message, I
simply need to be here, be present, and be conscious that
I am seated before God. An experience will come, embedded within her loving energy, within this light that shines so
brightly in front of me. I am tuned in to the light, my heart
open to the world of spirit, open to the light of God, open to
universal wisdom.

As I go deeper and deeper into the light, I embrace the
warmth that surrounds me. I am swimming in the very substance that is God. Listening to my surrounds, to this divine
light that fills my world, I pick up on any sounds, movements, or feelings coming from her light. In this alert, open
state, I am receptive to the full flow of God's silent, spiritual vibration. And as I listen, I continue to move deeper in,
deeper into God's light, until I am inside the light.

Here, resting quietly in the midst of her warm, uplifting light, I keep listening. And the more I listen, the more I
open myself up to and absorb the purity in my surrounds.
God is giving me what I need through her light, and
through the experience within her light. I am being given
full access to God's perfection, to her beauty. I surrender

entirely to the light and let God hold me, caress me, guide me. I let her embrace the child in me, and I feel her love warming every corner of my being.

## Journeying Home, Becoming Whole

Through the power of the mind and our imagination, we can travel to distant places without moving an inch. More than that, we can feel the presence of those in these faraway places too, meaning we have access to the entire world's population, right now. We can subtly touch whomever we wish to, wherever they may be, warming them with our vibration. All it takes is us directing our focused thoughts—and thus our energy—in their direction.

Similarly, a trip to the spiritual dimension is a mere thought away. All that's needed is the decision to take this journey, followed by intentional focus. We send our energy upward, zoom in, and watch in wonder as magic happens.

———

Sitting quietly, breathing gently, I watch as my body falls into fuzzy comfort. With my body settled, my mind automatically comes to the fore, and I become aware of its quiet, open space within. It is entirely nonphysical, this space—light and airy—and I realize that within this vast, untapped realm of my mind, I am truly unlimited. Here, I can free myself into the unknown, the unexplored, and experience things I never thought possible.

To experiment, I decide to go on the ultimate journey, to venture outward and upward, to move beyond all that is physical into the pure dimension of spirit. And that's what I do. By directing my thoughts to that higher world, my energy promptly takes me there. I am lifted upward, out of and beyond my body, and as quickly and simply as that, I find myself in an open space filled with light. I take a moment to accustom myself to my surrounds, and I sense the presence of a deep peace, a peace that has quite possibly existed here for eternity. This is God's home, after all: the land of silence and calm. And I feel God's resonance in that silence and calm.

I now visualize God as the spiritual sun, as the source of warmth, the source of divinity, the source of life and love. Seeing her before me, I seat myself comfortably in her sunlight, in the path of her energy, and I realize that I am, very naturally, meeting God. Her golden shimmer invites me closer and deeper into the expanse of her being. I allow myself to drift toward her light and into her clarity. She is coaxing me with love, and I follow that call. It's as though I am being invited to touch her light.

I do just that; I move into the brilliance of God's light and touch the splendor of her being. I touch her immaculate spirit, so untainted and complete, and my mind soars in the fullness and beauty of the moment. Here, surrounded by her energy, I am engulfed by a sense of homecoming. As God fills me with her warmth, I realize this is exactly where I want to be. Indeed, this is where I belong. This is my original home, a home infused with loving light. And God and I, we share a divine connection. We always did, and always will. Right now, I feel that connection intimately. Her energy surrounds me and enters me, lifts me, brings me into her and her into me. And as her spiritual light streams over me, into me, through me, I feel healing happening at some deep level within. I am being cleansed by the purest, most powerful light in existence. God's divine shimmer is soothing every cell in my body, touching every aspect of my being, restoring every fragment of my inner world with fresh, empowering energy. And with every moment spent in contact with this potent, giving light, with every passing second in the presence of God, renewal happens. I am being transformed by divinity.

As I go even deeper into the light, I feel myself being lifted further, healed more. I keep flowing inward, further and deeper into the light, until I find myself at the very center of God's existence. Here, seated within her radiance, I realize the impossible is possible. Anything I wish for, be it a feeling or experience, is available to me. Magic happens here, in the presence of sacred spirit. I am in touch with the sun, inside the source of all goodness, at the heart of the universe. I rest here, with God, and allow healing and renewal to continue their course in the most natural way. Here, in the presence of God, I am being made whole. I sit back and watch the wonder of transformation unfold.

## Bringing Down the Light

All paths lead to Rome, as they say—and likewise, a connection with God can be forged in many a colorful way. But if we were to distill the practice of connecting with the highest light into two approaches, we might conclude the following:

One, we can go up to God and enjoy a somewhat otherworldly experience with her in the spiritual realm.

Two, we can invite God down into our world, bringing her "otherworldliness" into our hearts and surrounds. Then, while carrying out our physical existence, we shower her light into our environment, splashing subtle beams of spiritual gold onto everything we do. This approach entails us becoming something of an intermediary between the spiritual and physical dimensions—or, to put it more romantically, an angel of light.

Let's apply this second method right now as we bring God's energy down to the people. Let's become those very angels of light.

———

I move my awareness to the core of my being, and into my heart I go. Here, I have access to the real me. Seated in my emotional and spiritual center, gazing around at all that is going on within me, I observe my inner workings. While I do so, I become aware of how comfortable I feel, seated here at the center of my being. There is a distinct absence of bustle—just a sweet, warm silence, a reassuring stillness.

As I continue to survey my quiet, inner surrounds, enjoying the peace within, I feel my heart beginning to grow. I feel it opening up, filling a wider and wider space within me. I breathe into this open expanse—a deep, slow, rejuvenating breath. As oxygen flows in, I witness a cleansing of my heart. I release my breath, then breathe in again, back into my heart-space, and I feel it opening wider still, become cleaner. And with each successive inhalation, I feel my heart inflating more, opening up so wide that the space of my heart extends across the expanse of my body. And now, from the center of my heart, I look upward to the supreme light. I direct my vision toward the universal source of inspiration and love. And there she is, that highest light, bright and full, beckoning me with her radiance. I focus on her mesmerizing glow, simply appreciating the might, the richness, the beauty of her presence. It's time, though, to bring her energy down to the earth. And so, very consciously, I invite her light into me, into my open heart, and immediately sense her rays being channeled my way. I feel her energy funneling into and filling the vast space of my heart, and I welcome its vigor.

As her light flows in, touching the deepest parts of my being, it's as though a majestic fire, warm and pure, has ignited within. It spreads its golden influence into the farthest reaches of my being. I feel God's loving embrace filling me from within. I feel her glow: a light that is strong, a force filled with healing energy. I let this light intensify and sweep through me, cleaning me, lifting me, loving me. And now, I let this light filter out into my surrounds. I observe a grand arc of light spreading out from my heart in all directions around me. I sit back and let it shine. I let my heart and the light of God within me radiate outward. It's this simple letting go, this conscious releasing of the light, that allows my light and God's to nourish those in my surrounds; I am letting them too be lifted by its magnificence.

Having stepped into my role as an angel of inspiration, I walk forward into this day, fueled by the highest spiritual light. Beauty opens up around me. I am filled with the purity and simplicity of divine light, an instrument of the universal spirit, a shining beacon for the world. I am that flowing angel, helping others to touch, and be touched, by God's exquisite light.

## Turning My Face to the Sun

As humans, we have a natural attraction toward light, instinctively knowing all the benefits embedded in its healthy glow. Simply *visualizing* light is enough to attune us to that world of cleansing, empowering energy. Light also lulls us into contented states; just the thought of lying back on a sofa, blanketed in warm beams of winter sun, is guaranteed to boost our mood!

Let's open ourselves up, both physically and spiritually, to the nourishing properties of light. Let's fill ourselves with its natural goodness as we allow it to infiltrate the length and breadth of our being.

I close my eyes and tilt my head toward the cool darkness of the ground below. I take a moment to really feel that coolness reflected off the ground, to experience its refreshing inward flow. I enjoy the placid nature of the darkness, too, as it seeps into me, spreading its stillness. I now inhale, and as I do so, I breathe in more of this dark, tranquil, soft energy. Following its soothing flow into my body, I become aware of my own cool, shadowed space within. I spend a minute just resting in this inner space, taking pleasure from my own silent, private world. All is at peace inside me, a gentle calm lingering in the air. The darkness is good, but its polar opposite, light, is even better. And so, to invite in brightness, I begin to tilt my face—very slowly, inch by inch—upward.

As I do so, I notice—through closed eyes—a gradual illuminating of my surrounds. And as I continue turning my eyes upward, I sense a dazzling glow somewhere up above. It's a welcoming light, pulling me in its direction. I accept the invitation of this pull and simply surrender to its influence. I allow myself to be drawn closer to the light, closer to its radiance, closer to its reassuring glow. I want to share in its beauty, to touch its fullness. I want to be with this light. I continue angling my face toward the light, feeling a magnetic pull emanating from this ball of bright energy as it draws me toward its warm center. Still, I continue tilting my face upward, hungrily yet patiently anticipating more warmth, more light. Feeling these beams of energy lighting up my cheeks, I sense contentment bubbling up in me, erupting in a warm smile breaking out across the breadth of my face.

My eyes are now aimed directly upward. Looking straight into this loving light, I feel my forehead catch its uplifting, warm energy, absorbing it into that once-dark space inside my body. I am being lit up, my interior now radiant with a proliferation of golden light descending onto and into me. I sense how my entire being is orientated toward the light. My limbs, my core, my mind, and my heart all face this glow of pure energy in front of me, its beams of light streaming onto me, into me, through me.

As I continue to absorb the light, I feel myself being lifted more and more toward its center, toward the very source of this light. A deep love for the light surfaces in me, and it is now patently clear this is so much more than mere light. This is God before me, drawing me in, showing me beauty in its purest, original form.

Here, standing directly in front of the awe-inspiring radiance that is God, I have entered a force field of the highest, most transformative energy. And with her stream of light entering me, I feel the commencement of healing—healing of the warmest, richest, deepest kind. It's a healing replete with love both tangible and real, a love that fills my being. I feel the magic of love coursing through me, lighting up and restoring my being. My entire body vibrates as it catches the light and beams with the fullness of spiritual might. Simply being here, being conscious, being open, I am forging a life-changing connection with the highest, most divine light.

## Taking a Walk with God

Nature has a way of drawing us into reflective moods; just think how easily and naturally we slip into meditative states while walking on a soft, sandy beach or along a serene forest path.

What follows is precisely one such walking meditation through nature, with the presence of warm sunlight being the catalyst for comfort and growth.

Walking in nature, I feel the gorgeous glint of sunshine streaming down onto me. With my body bathed in gold, I survey the fresh beauty of my surrounds, and I automatically sense my pace slowing down, my body relaxing. The sheer comfort of it all lulls me into a calm, reflective state, and I become conscious of each step I take. My footsteps are soft and gentle, delicately touching the surface of the earth.

While moving forward, I take in the fullness of my environment, of the prolific greenery and the profusion of life. I notice the effect the crisp sunlight is having on each element of nature, every beam of light brightening and coloring my surrounds with magic. I shift my focus back to myself, back to the feeling of sunlight spreading its warmth across my body. My skin is like a sponge, soaking up the golden shafts of light, taking their healthy glow deep into my body. This sunlight feels so pure, its energy so essential; I could easily imagine it to be a deeper kind of light, a light from another dimension.

And I let it be that; this liberal stream of light, filling my being with its warmth, is indeed a sacred, otherworldly light. It is the light originating from that higher dimension, from the realm of spirit. It is a light that, although having crossed over into our dimension, still carries all the magic of its original home. It is the light of God, and right now I am the instrument attracting this ethereal light toward the earth. I have enabled God's light to travel from the spiritual plane down into our physical plane. I am the magnet drawing the light into our world. I feel the purity of these rays as they touch me, warm me, enter me.

There is something very special about this light, about the way it feels as it flows into me. Yes, this is divine light. Without question, this is a light that comes from some hallowed space of purity and peace. And although this light comes from an entirely different dimension, I have direct access to its magnificence. This light hovering over me is the light of God, after all, and I feel her presence as though she were right beside me. As I continue to walk forward, I notice I am moving even closer toward this great, ethereal being. With each step, I am approaching the origin of beauty. With each step, I am moving toward God's light, making it more real, more vibrant, more empowering. Each step takes me deeper and higher. And even as I continue to keep my eyes on the physical path up ahead, my spiritual vision is locked solely on God's light, locked into the center of her glow. And the more I focus on her essence, the more I feel like I am ascending, becoming stronger.

With every step, I am absorbing more light, more clarity, more truth. I am becoming more of what I want to be. As I move forward, I am moving deeper into my higher self. By keeping my sights set on God alone, I am allowing her light to polish me, to complete me, to enlighten me. God's guiding presence knows precisely what I need in this moment. I just have to trust the light, follow the light, allow the light to clean me. I simply need to surrender to the transformative power of God's energy. Her warmth continues to enter me, filling my inner being with its steady, rich flow. It lights up all my dark spaces, illuminating my world from within. And as this light settles inside me, it becomes part of me. A distinct feeling of being composed entirely of light fills me. My basic substance, my inner foundation, is light. I have been swallowed by radiance.

Now, to express the beauty of this moment, to offer my appreciation, I raise my palms to this perfect sun hovering up ahead and give thanks. With hands aloft, I draw more of God's essence into my being and feel myself being nudged toward bliss. I am touching the sun, and the sun is touching me. I walk and live in the light. I am one with the spiritual sun, and the sun's light fills me, moves me, transforms me. My connection with the higher spiritual dimension is a direct one, and I bring its inherent beauty and peace down into our world, into my surrounds, into this moment. I walk forward, always toward the light, always with the light, always filled with the purity of the highest light.

## Summoning the Upward Surge

As much as we'd all love for our lives to be a flowing river of positivity and bliss, there are times when we feel run-down or lack the confidence, strength, or willpower to move forward. In moments like these, what's needed is a surge of power to get us back on track and rekindle our enthusiasm, clarity, and vision.

"One espresso—and make it a double, please!"

Caffeine may help, but—as is so often the case—there are spiritual solutions, too: spiritual *surges*, which are both on tap and bottomless, just like our coffee!

The two obvious kinds of spiritual energy available to us are the energy of the soul and that of God. Regarding our own spiritual energy, because it exists right here inside us, it's constantly no more than an inward glance away. It's here, always, nestled warmly in our hearts. Admittedly, it's subtle. But if we choose to look for it, it can feel tangible and rich. By directing our vision inward with the intention of locating our inner light, we can be certain that the soul—our deep, conscious, living energy—will make itself known to us, perhaps as a warm glow, a bright light, or just as a general fullness of being. By focusing specifically on the energy within the soul and on its explosive potential—remember, we're talking about accessing power—we can ignite it. We can release its might into our inner world, boosting us and giving us, precisely, that upward surge.

Importantly, we needn't limit such power surges to low-energy days alone; when we're feeling optimistic and our spirits are high, inducing this inner upwelling of energy can take us straight into bliss. The impossible, in that moment, will feel truly possible—and easy, too. We can fill ourselves with such spiritual power that we'll be virtually bursting with the vigor and beauty of the moment as light and might stream out from every pore. We can have fun with this inner surge, too, experimenting with just how high we can go. The result is a kind of cleansing burn, a way upward—*fast*.

The second energy, that of God, has the same if not more potential for igniting our world. Although otherworldly, this energy can be as warm and close as our best friend, resting not just beside us, but *inside* us, too. This is the energy we'll be delving into in the following meditation as we go on a quest for that fully-fledged upward surge via God's awe-inspiring light.

Let's cast our eyes up to the higher dimension and get seriously high on light.

Sitting here, very quietly, I go in search of inspiration. I look for that bolt of life that will propel me forward and upward, that will give me the momentum to make the seemingly impossible possible, that will allow me to reach my dreams and touch bliss. I look to the higher plane for that flash of light, for that pulse of electricity, for that vital life. I direct my focus solely toward the essence-full light above, toward that being of shimmering gold who shines constantly. I see her—God, no less—in front of me. And I do more than look at her light—I look *into* her light.

Her glow is directly in front of me, and I hold my gaze firmly on her, witnessing and feeling the power before me. I allow myself to be drawn closer toward this clean-burning fire that is the universal source of goodness, of wholeness, of vigor. And still closer I go toward her radiant, molten energy, toward this force that is capable of incinerating all negativity in an instant. Here, standing directly before God's light, I feel enriched, empowered, full. And now, to enable an experience of intense purification, I take one final step forward and find myself inside God's light.

As I enter her vast, dazzling force field, I feel myself being rocked by her presence. I feel the full might of God. A surge of power streams into me—God's light funneling in—and the rush of her strength stirs me, fills me, heals me with her cleansing force. I sit within this surge—just sit and accept all, giving myself over to everything that is divine and powerful. I hand myself over to God and let my world be uplifted, transformed, and purified by her might. Light torrents in, and I feel my entire being vibrating with the formidable presence of God's energy inside me. Here, all I need to do is sit back and let it happen—let her intensity and beauty enter me, fill me, flow through me.

With every passing moment spent in the presence of this immense, spirit-filled light, I feel myself becoming stronger, more focused, more capable of reaching the highest me. As God's molten energy continues its inward flow, I observe the way my entire being is pulsing with divinity. The light burns within, and the burn is good, and pure, and satisfying. The burn is healing. I feel the essence of God's spirit filling and renewing me, transforming me into exactly who I want to be.

## Guided by the Light

By staying connected to God's light as we weave our way through life, we quickly discover a positive perspective blossoming inside us—with little or no effort, other than holding on to that subtle thread of divine light, of course!

Let's say yes to that natural boost as we tune in to God's guiding light.

———

Sitting quietly, breathing gently, I turn my vision gently upward. And there, before my eyes—manifested as a glowing energy, a beacon of warm light—I find God. With a kind of calm wonder, I notice my heart opening to this light and my gaze filling with love. I realize it's the beauty in the light that is triggering this blossoming of soft emotion in me. I feel an indescribable closeness to this special being before me, as well as an overwhelming sense of wanting to experience more of her beauty, to explore more of her light. No sooner have I had this thought than I am being pulled effortlessly forward and upward toward her light.

All of a sudden, it's so clear: this is destiny. I am simply meant to be here, with this clean shimmer that is God. I am inseparably connected to her. Our bond is eternal. We share some deep, mysterious relationship that can never be broken. And so it is that I move naturally in, toward the very center of this being. I am overcome with a feeling of warmth here, so inviting is her presence.

As I venture deeper into God's light, I understand God's essence more clearly. I see more of her purity, feel more of her love. I am calm in the presence of all this beauty, still in the presence of her light. As her light beams out around me, strength starts to filter into my world, and I notice growth happening in me, right now. Just by placing myself here in front of God's light and by inviting the presence of this extraordinary being into my world, I have opened the gates to transformation. I have enabled God to do what she wishes to do—to caress me and guide me toward a life of meaning and beauty. All that's needed is for me to seat myself before her with a heart open and receptive to the energy she wishes to pass on to me.

I now take a slow breath in, into my belly, and as I breathe out, I surrender to God. I give myself over, diving fully into her light, into her radiance, into her depth. I go into God's world, and in an instant, my surrounds are flooded with light. I have entered the profundity of her wisdom, the fullness of her power. Here, having released myself into the light, I allow God to touch me in the deepest way—in a way only God can. With her divine presence beside me, with me, in me, I feel the magnitude of God's embrace in all its full, unconditional, all-encompassing splendor. She fills me with her light, her vibration, her love. I feel her energy seeping into me, and my entire being glows in response.

All of a sudden, I notice something special happening: light has started shining out from me, too, in an aura rich with substance and strength. I inherently know that this is an aura that, in surrounding me with divinity, will shield me from negativity. It's God's light, after all, being reflected through me. I walk forward into the day, encased in a bright energy that encircles me, moves me, loves me. I am walking within the light, and the light embraces me. I allow God to guide me, to fuel me, to protect me. I am one with the highest, most perfect light. And though I exist in the physical world, I hold on to my connection with the realm of subtle light.

# Chapter 12
# Reflections

And that, dear friends, concludes our compendium of 101 meditations. But wait ... there's more! One more. This final meditation is designed to keep us on our journey toward personal discovery and truth, via the medium of self-reflective questions. Its premise is that if we keep asking probing questions, we're bound to stumble upon consequential answers.

Let's enjoy that process of self-inquiry as we head off in search of those hidden treasures within.

## Contemplations in the Presence of Light

When we combine self-reflection with remembrance of God, incredible things happen. We open up pathways to the highest wisdom, and spiritual realizations are bound to surface. Such realizations can change the way we look at and experience life—in an unequivocally positive, and often very practical way.

For this magic to happen, we simply require an attitude of curiosity and openness, as well as the patience to *listen*. We need to venture out with an inquisitive yet trusting heart as we engage with God, inviting her wisdom into our world. She *is* the one who understands what we need right now, after all.

Let's open up our hearts and tune in to the highest intelligence. Let's ask some deep questions about existence, then listen carefully for the response.

———

I tilt my head, my mind, my energy upward, knowing God is there. Knowing that her loving light is gently watching over me, that she is inviting me to move toward her light. I realize I often forget to open myself up to this divine invitation, thus missing the opportunity to reunite with beauty's origin, with the purest light in existence, with the light that heals, nourishes, and offers wisdom. To afford myself the privilege of this connection, I now reach out to God.

As I touch the light, I feel her warmth trickle into me, caressing me as it begins to fill me. And still I keep my gaze focused on God. I direct my energy toward the center of her light now, knowing that everything I need, right now, is contained within this light. I take the light in, absorbing its purity, making it part of me. I let the light enter my cells, my heart, my being. And deeper into her light I go, venturing to the very source. I am surrounded by God's light now, and I trust the warmth I feel here. I trust the power. It is tangible, this warmth, this power. It exists as a force around me and influences me in a resoundingly positive way.

Now, seated within the fullness of the light, knowing that God's transcendent presence holds the deepest wisdom, I choose to reflect on my existence. I frame my reflections as questions, and then—in the company of God—I listen for the response. Looking into God's light, I ask,

"What do I need, right now? What experience would make me truly happy?"

As I ask this question, I hold God's presence in front of me. I feel God's luminescence surrounding me. Now, listening for answers, I let her wisdom enter me via her light, via a possible experience embedded in her light. I rest here, listening for the hints of a response. If necessary, I repeat the question, and listen again, until a degree of clarity has emerged.

I approach this meditation with the utmost patience. By asking the question in the presence of God, by giving myself the time to truly merge into God's light as I listen for a response, as I feel for a response, I will find clarity. This is *my* time to seek truth. This is *my* time in communion with God. By opening myself up in this way and contemplating aspects of significance in the midst of God's light, I am invoking answers, very likely via an experience. With every question asked in the presence of God, with every moment spent listening to that presence, I can progress rapidly and accurately.

When I feel I've made progress regarding my first inquiry, I can move on to another aspect of my life I wish to better understand, via the next question:

"What is the state of my heart right now?"

While gazing into God's light, I ask question after question, pausing patiently and listening carefully after each one.

"What is a clean heart? Is my heart as clean as I wish it to be? How do I go about cleansing my heart?"

"Is my heart open now? Do I generally live with an open heart? What does that feel like? How can I open it more?"

"Am I being true to myself? Are there areas in my life where I could be more honest in my expression?"

"Is there anything I am hiding within that I could bring out into the open, right now, to lighten my load?"

"What scares me? Is this fear rational? How can I overcome it?"

"Am I taking care of myself? How could I look after myself better?"

"Do I love myself? How can I love myself more?"

"Am I in control of my life? If not, how can I regain control? What mental exercise could I practice to take back control?"

"What makes me the happiest? How can I go about doing more of the things that make me happy?"

"What is most important to me in life? Do I spend enough time appreciating and cultivating it? How can I bring more of it into my life?"

"What advice could I give myself, now?"

"What aspect of my life could I improve? How can I bring about those improvements?"

"In what facets of my life do I really shine? How can I place more emphasis on these facets, enabling them to bring more light into both my life and the lives of others?"

"Who am I, really? Am I revealing who I want to be? How could I reveal more of the being I wish to be?"

"If this moment were perfect, what would it feel like?"

"Sitting here, how can I spread love into the world? Can I do that, now?"

"How am I doing spiritually? How can I bring more spirituality into my life? How deeply can I go into a spiritual experience, right now?"

"What does it mean to fully let go? Am I able to do that now—just let go?"

"What does the hush of true silence feel like? Can I hear it now?"

"How does a subtle entity like the soul express its power? What does it feel like when I express that power?"

"What does it mean and feel like to be enlightened? Can I step into that feeling now?"

"What does it mean and feel like to be eternal?"

"Who are you, God? How can I come closer to you?"

"In what aspects am I, the soul, similar to God?"

"What would it feel like to have a full experience of you, God? Can I invite that experience now?"

I continue studying God's light, peering deeply into its warm radiance. As I do so, I feel her immaculate flow entering me while I ponder the intricacies of living and of loving. And as I explore my fullness of being in the presence of divine light, I develop a deeper understanding of all aspects of myself and of my relationship with this miracle called life.

# Conclusion

And so, dear readers, we come to the end of our pilgrimage, having meandered our way through ~~101~~ 102 pathways of the mind. But an ending, of course, is merely the signal of new beginnings. Let's actively engage this newness as we head out today, continuing our inward and upward path on this mystical journey of life.

And as we look out through these eyes at the wonders of the world, let's remain mindful of our inner spark of consciousness. Let's embrace abundance as we invite the brilliance of spirituality into our everyday actions. Let's enjoy the simple pleasures that sprout from doing simple actions while living consciously. Let's breathe slowly and deeply, centering ourselves as we connect to spirit.

I thank you all for accompanying me on this journey toward realization and truth via the colorful path of meditation. I wish you every success in your spiritual pursuits. Keep looking within. Keep finding those answers that lie solely in the realm of experience. And as you do so, may you continue living a life filled with happiness, healing, and love.

And lastly, if you have any questions or comments, hearing from you would make my day! Drop me a line, anytime, at meditate withmurray@gmail.com.

Yours, in the fullness of peace,

Murray

## To Write to the Author

If you wish to contact the author or would like more information about this book, please write to the author in care of Llewellyn Worldwide Ltd. and we will forward your request. Both the author and the publisher appreciate hearing from you and learning of your enjoyment of this book and how it has helped you. Llewellyn Worldwide Ltd. cannot guarantee that every letter written to the author can be answered, but all will be forwarded. Please write to:

Murray du Plessis
℅ Llewellyn Worldwide
2143 Wooddale Drive
Woodbury, MN 55125-2989

Please enclose a self-addressed stamped envelope for reply, or $1.00 to cover costs. If outside the U.S.A., enclose an international postal reply coupon.

Many of Llewellyn's authors have websites with additional information and resources. For more information, please visit our website at http://www.llewellyn.com.

# Notes

# Notes

_____

_____

_____

_____

_____

_____

_____

_____

_____

_____

_____

_____

_____

_____

_____

# Notes

_____

_____

_____

_____

_____

_____

_____

_____

_____

_____

_____

_____

_____

_____

_____

# Notes

_____

_____

_____

_____

_____

_____

_____

_____

_____

_____

_____

_____

_____

_____

# Notes